Goddess Has Answers to Life's Tough Problems

Wiccans—How You Can Experience Happiness and Healing through Goddess's Wisdom

from GoddessHasYourBack.com

Moonwater SilverClaw

Wiccan High Priestess
Blogger/Founder of
GoddessHasYourBack.com
with visitors from 191 countries

A QuickBreakthrough Publishing Edition

Copyright © 2019 Johanna Ellen Mac Leod
ISBN-13: 978-0998427331

All rights reserved. No part of this book may be reproduced or transmitted in any form by any means electronic or mechanical, including photocopying, recording or by any information storage and retrieval system without written permission from the publisher.

More copies are available from the publisher with the imprint QuickBreakthrough Publishing. For more information about this book contact: askawitchnow@gmail.com

This book was developed and written with care. Names and details were modified to respect privacy.

Disclaimer: The author and publisher acknowledge that each person's situation is unique, and that readers have full responsibility to seek consultations with health, financial, spiritual and legal professionals. The author and publisher make no representations or warranties of any kind, and the author and publisher shall not be liable for any special, consequential or exemplary damages resulting, in whole or in part, from the reader's use of, or reliance upon, this material.:

Other Books by Moonwater SilverClaw:
- Goddess Has Your Back
- Goddess Style Weight Loss
- Goddess Walks Beside You
- Break Free with Goddess
- The Hidden Children of the Goddess
- Be a Wiccan Badass
- Beyond the Law of Attraction to Real Magick
- Goddess Reveals Your Enchanted Light

Praise for Moonwater SilverClaw:

• "Moonwater was telling me about her weight loss program and it sounded like something I could do that didn't cost me more than the normal groceries I buy, anyway. I started with an egg omelet in the morning with mushrooms and spinach. ... In two weeks, I lost 7 lbs. I had a couple of days of eating what I wanted but not overeating. Then right back to **Goddess Style**. I feel great and eat what the Goddess gives us." – Denise Kopplinger

• "In her book *The Hidden Children of the Goddess*, Moonwater brings Wicca to life, enveloping you in the mystery and magick of the Craft. Her writing talent is amazing! Her kindness and even sense of fun is ever present throughout her writing. Moonwater expresses profound Wicca concepts through examples in her own life experience. Wicca actually saved her life. and empowered her to leave an abusive marriage, and this shows the power of this sacred path to positively change the course of our lives, too. Moonwater's stories personally inspire me, and I am confident that they will inspire you also." – Rev. Patrick McCollum, internationally recognized spiritual leader working for human rights, social justice, and equality; the 2010 recipient of the Mahatma Gandhi Award for the Advancement of Pluralism.

• "Religion scholars in the future will likely view Moonwater SilverClaw as the pivotal voice that helped change the discourse on Wicca. In her book **Goddess Has Your Back,** Moonwater reveals Wicca as a very positive and ultimately uplifting spirituality choice. She demystifies the religion's taboos and spooky stereotypes through her unintimidating presentation that clarifies the topic. She introduces the Goddess and the magick rituals that, when used properly, can positively impact your everyday life. The author relays her very personal perspective on the subject and shows how to integrate the philosophies and practices of the centuries-old religion. Looking for a fresh perspective on spiritual growth? Read what Moonwater SilverClaw has to say." – Stacy D. Horn

• "Moonwater's writing will give you a portrait of a woman who lives her faith, and whose life was saved by it. Because so many lives, my own included, were irrevocably changed by Wicca, were given new focus, new purpose, and perhaps most importantly, new personal power to realize one's dreams and ambitions.... It's a story about making your own happy endings, about rescuing yourself...." – Jason Pitzl-Waters, former blogger at WildHunt.org

Visit Moonwater's blog: www.GoddessHasYourBack.com

CONTENTS*
These are highlights. There is much more material in this book!

Acknowledgments		I
Section 1: You Are Loved and Valued		1
Section 2: Not Yet		29
Section 3: This is not safe		55
Section 4: Yes, you can grow even when it feels scary		95
Section 5: Come home to Me		131
Candle Ritual and Putting Up a Shield		91
About the Author; Special Offer to Reader of this Book		165,166
About Online Course *Goddess Style Weight Loss*		164
Excerpt from *Goddess Has Your Back*		166
Excerpt from *Beyond the Law of Attraction to Real Magick*		169

DEDICATION AND ACKNOWLEDGMENTS

This book is dedicated to the God and Goddess. Thanks to Tom Marcoux for editing. Thanks to Kay Pannell for her guidance and friendship.

Thank you and blessings to you, the reader.

GoddessHasYourBack.com

For insights about spells, rituals, and more
Visit GoddessHasYourBack.com
for blog posts and to sign up for
Moonwater SilverClaw's E-newsletter.

Goddess Has Answers for You

Goddess has answers for life's tough problems. What does this mean? It means that Wiccans across the years have experienced, through ritual, meditation and quiet moments, flashes of insight and intuition. In these ways, they have received Goddess's answers. This book will share with you, rituals, guidance, prayers and meditations so that you can open the door. Now, you can invite Goddess to give you the answers to the life's tough problems when you need them.

Section 1

Goddess Answers, "You Are Loved and Valued."

In conversations with other Wiccans, I've discovered so many of us ask these questions:
- Will I ever feel okay?
- Will I ever have confidence?

- Will someone comfort me?
- Will someone validate me?

Perhaps, you're like me, and you might feel that you've started with some stuff that holds you back. I have dyslexia asthma and clinical depression. At times in my life, I thought I just didn't have what it takes to *just survive* or to even approach the possibility of feeling fulfilled and happy.

Do you feel that you're under some form of disadvantage?

If so, I'm with you.

I went through years of pain. Finally, during a particular meditation session, **I had a direct experience of Goddess's love.**

In this experience, I felt the presence of the Goddess and God right beside me. The word that hints as what I felt is *acceptance.* **It was an experience of being loved, accepted and cherished for the first time in my life.** When you have such an experience with Goddess, much of *your uncertainty quiets down.* It doesn't go completely away, but it is a blessing to know that the Goddess and God are present.

They care about you.

In this section we're going to talk about different aspects of having the deep knowing that you are loved and valued.

You Are Loved and Valued #1

Goddess Is the Source of Your Certainty

"Why is it getting worse?" my friend, Stephanie, said.

"I know there's a lot happening. Anything in particular?" I replied.

"More violence in this country!" Stephanie said. And, this

began a significant conversation.

What if Goddess Serves as Your Source of Certainty?

Is it possible to be certain of anything, anymore? Some people complain, "Unbelievable. I could *not* even imagine that people in leadership positions would be so ... disgusting."

I've learned that there is value in seeing ourselves as "spiritual beings having a human experience."

As many of my constant readers know, I believe in the Summerlands, a place of love and peace in between the times we incarnate. We return and incarnate into a new body, and the lessons begin. We use our bodies as a user-interface for our spiritual being to learn lessons on this physical plane.

I realize that it can be tough to see this spiritual level when we're in the midst of suffering and confusion. It's as if we're wearing "human-tinted glasses." I suggest that we pause and consider looking at our lives from Goddess's perspective. Goddess knows.

A Source of Comfort

Sometimes, I return to *The Charge of the Goddess* for inspiration and comfort.

"Let my worship be within the heart that rejoiceth, for behold: all acts of love and pleasure are my rituals. And therefore, let there be beauty and strength, power and compassion, honor and humility, mirth and reverence within you." – Doreen Valiente (speaking in the voice of the Goddess—from The Charge of the Goddess)

A couple of meanings rise for me with the above quote.

Notice the phrase "all acts of love and pleasure are my rituals," and see that the Goddess gives us the answer. We can derive comfort in honoring Her with our compassion, reverence, humility and more. Acts of kindness and beauty honor the Goddess and make us feel good.

A Prayer
Dear Goddess
Release me from my stale, limited beliefs
And give me compassion and mirth in heaps.
Acts of love and Acts of pleasure.
I honor You in this way forever.

May the ideas expressed here comfort you and invite you to listen to your heart. May compassion for others flourish in your heart.

You Are Loved and Valued #2

How do I Create a Wiccan Daily Practice?

Often, I'm asked about how Wiccans can really support their relationship with God and Goddess and deepen their Wiccan spiritual practice.

I often share **The Three Elements to Improve Your Wiccan Practice.**

1. What do you want to accomplish?
The whole point in much of Wicca is being close to the Gods. All the ritual we do, all the meditating we do—it's about getting to the ecstatic state of being closer to the Source.

Do you want to start a meditation practice? Or how about doing more rituals each week? In creating a daily practice, you first have to figure out what you're going to do.

Maybe you want to hone your magickal skills.

Here's the first thing to consider: Start with something easy. Avoid setting yourself up to fail.

Start with something simple. You could do a simple

candle lighting ceremony, for example.

2. How much time do you have?

Here's the good news: Whatever time you have, you can make your Wiccan spiritual practice better.

Some examples:

1 minute – say a prayer or chant (out loud)

3 to 5 minutes – Have a brief meditation session.

30 minutes – Do a simple ritual. Perhaps, include a candle lighting ceremony and some meditation.

1 hour – Do a formal ritual.

The more time you have, the more you can do. Just remember to pace yourself.

Even if you have only a short time to spare, you can still get big benefits. How? Practice will help you hone whatever skill/discipline you are trying to work with.

Even doing a three-minute meditation session will bring you results over time.

3. How will you log it?

Logging your practice is crucial. If you do not log your actions, you really don't know if you're making any progress.

Some people use a diary. Diaries are great to log what you did, the duration of your practice, and what the outcome was.

What if you don't like to write? No problem. You can use your smartphone to record your progress. You can pick an app to log your efforts.

Otherwise, you can simply mark a paper-based calendar on the days you successfully complete your practice.

Wiccans also find that having another Wiccan as your "accountability buddy" helps.

* * * * * *

In summary, you can accomplish much even with a short time—when you do things daily. Use *The Three Elements to Improve Your Wiccan Practice.*

May this process help you.

You Are Loved and Valued #3

Real Comfort for Wiccans—Talking to the Gods

"I've got this lump in my breast," I said to my husband. Shook up, he sat down in a chair. He'd been through the breast cancer journey with his mother. He had to hold her hand while she was having a lumpectomy under local anesthetic.

This was the beginning of my health-related journey.

My husband usually asks, "Would you consider doing ___?" But when he heard about the lump in my breast he said, "We need some other way of talking. I'm asking that you to do something other than 'consider.' Would you please take immediate action? Okay?"

I called at 7 AM the next morning to make an appointment. The staff took the situation seriously and set up my appointment at 2:30 pm that same day.

1. Communication with God and Goddess

As I drove to my appointment I prayed and asked the God and Goddess for Their input.

Suddenly I felt calm inside as They answered, "It's not cancer."

Still, the doctor examined me and said, "I don't know what that mass is. Time for you to get your first mammogram."

2. Communication with People

When I got home, I told my husband that I didn't think it was anything and told him not to worry. I learned later that my comment provided him with no relief from his worries. He later said, "I would have appreciated if you had told me that you had communicated with the God and Goddess. Why? Because when you said, 'I think'… I didn't know what that was. Maybe you might have been in denial."

Telling people you love what's going on is important. I could have relieved my husband from much of his burden of worry by just letting him know what the God and Goddess told me.

Ultimately, I had both a mammogram and an ultrasound test.

The results? Benign cysts.

Phew!

Still, I'm invited by my doctor to continue monitoring the situation.

In summary, remember to make good efforts to communicate with both the Gods and your loved ones.

You Are Loved and Valued #4

Secret Desires that Draw Wiccans to the Craft

"Why did you become a witch?" Lena, a friend, asked me.

This started my thoughts about how many of us, Wiccans, find our way to this spiritual path.

I note four related topics:
- You want control over your life
- You don't like being told what to believe
- You love the Old Gods
- You want to learn Secret Knowledge

1. You want control over your own life

Many witches want the power to control their own lives. This draws them to magick.

Several individuals find their way to witchcraft because they feel that their life is out of control, and they feel the need to create the world they want.

You may desire a better job, home or a new lover. (Be careful of love spells. You only want to remove blocks to love *in yourself*.)

We note that to gain a job, one needs to do mundane practices boosted by magick. Mundane?—yes, we send out resumes and go to networking events.

Magick can help us weave our own destinies—at least the parts we can influence. Magick courses through us and the world around us. Witches harness these energies to change those things they need to influence. Numerous witches perform spells for those things they desire.

Using spells, witches can control their lives in ways others cannot.

2. You don't like being told what to believe

Along with having control of your life comes the fact that a witch doesn't like being told what to think and what to believe.

We are free thinkers. We don't blindly follow some priest in a church. We don't blindly follow a priest's pronouncements. We question authority.

Wicca attracts many women who celebrate that women have equal rights and powers as men.

Furthermore, many women have already had experiences with the paranormal. (Men have paranormal encounters, too.) For example, I observed Shadow People and heard a poltergeist while growing up in a haunted home.

Like others, I have wanted answers to such unusual occurrences.

3. You love the Old Gods

During my childhood, my parents dragged me to their Christian Church. I couldn't relate to their version of an angry, father-figure God who apparently doesn't like people!

I wanted to interact with a god who wasn't angry or

punishing. My intuition told me that there were other Gods to interact with.

Some of us grew up reading the ancient myths of different cultures and falling in love with the Gods of old. One of my good friends had such an experience.

As a child, I found myself naturally doing rituals. I gathered berries and made a little altar, somewhat near my home. This was possible since I grew up in an undeveloped area of Redwood City, California.

When I read about Wicca some years later, I realized that I was already doing ritual. I found myself attracted to the Goddess and the Horned God.

4. You want to learn Secret Knowledge

Once we've begun our Wiccan journey and we're practicing as solitary witches, some of us wanted to learn the deep secrets of magick and the Wiccan Path.

Many witches realize that they want to practice as a solitary. Still, for the deepest knowledge, one can get initiated into one of the Traditions. This is an interesting transition. Why? Many of us begin with *not* wanting to be told what to do. However, in going through the secret training of the seeker, you do find that to stay safe while doing magick, you need to follow precise directions. Hopefully, by this point, the witch is *not* overly concerned about taking direction—because she or he is more focused on diving deep into the Secret Knowledge.

My own training, over years, led to my earning the role of 3rd Degree High Priestess of the Gardnerian Tradition. In the Gardnerian Tradition, there is much Secret Knowledge that I cannot even hint about in my blog.

Once initiated, one discovers a whole new world of information. We note that newly initiated witches dive deep, clamoring for more and deeper secret knowledge. Only initiated witches receive the specific *Book of Shadows* (BOS) of the particular Tradition. The BOS unveils the secrets of the Gods and the Craft, satiating the thirst for knowledge.

In summary, many of us, Wiccans, come to our spiritual path because of these details:
- You want control over your life
- You don't like being told what to believe
- You love the Old Gods
- You want to learn Secret Knowledge

Many blessings on your journey.

You Are Loved and Valued #5

How Wicca Rocks!

Unlike some religions, Wicca is *not* shut down like it's a little thing hiding in a bunker.

I'll say it: *Wicca rocks.*

This became clear to me as I answered another question posed by a reader at Quora.com

The reader asked me "Can I practice Wicca and Be a Buddhist?" I answered as follows:

"To reply to your question, I had a conversation with a college professor who taught Comparative Religion for 14 years.

Our conversation provided many insights.

Here's a partial list:

1. Buddhism separates into several sects.

Different sects of Buddhism have different requirements. So, our conversation here will be about Buddhism in general. For many Buddhism practitioners, this path often functions like a philosophy. The Buddha is *not* considered a "god"—he was a human being who, through diligent effort, became enlightened. In fact, Buddha, as a name, means "enlightened."

2. Buddhism and Wicca have concepts that relate to each other (karma and "The 3-Fold Law" also known as "The Law of Three")

To quote a post I did for my blog GoddessHasYourBack.com:

"Let's talk about the Law of Three, or the threefold law of return. Whatever energy you send out into the universe will get magnified three-fold and then returned to you. It is a simple principle. But when we observe this principle in action, it proves complex.

Imagine that we have a pond which we'll call the "universe pond." You have some stones in your pocket. The stones represent the actions you take in life and in turn, the energy you send out into the universe arising from those actions.

You drop a stone into the pond. Ripples move out from the stone's entry point to the pond.

As energy created from your action, the ripples spread into the universe and grow in magnitude. Eventually, they hit the edge of the pond and bounce back to you in their magnified form.

So, the stone you dropped in the pond, (an action you took in the universe, whether it was a positive action or a negative one,) comes back to you. Just like nature, the universe has a self-regulating system, many people call this Karma.

So carefully choose your actions.

May the ripples return to you three-fold in positive energy."

Buddhism's focus on karma relates to "cause and effect." (We can see the similarity with The Law of Three.)

One creates karma by one's actions. You can pay for your misdeeds in this life or in the next life (see reincarnation below). Some people talk about thinking a bad thought and then stubbing their toe as "instant karma." That might strike someone as amusing. Still, several people talk about "I was kind to that person and later they helped me get a job." Therefore, karma is *not* only about being good now so that your later incarnation will turn out well.

So, as you can see, Wicca and Buddhism appear to have some beliefs that line up—in a way.

3. Buddhism and Wicca have compatibility with the concepts "loving kindness" and "An it harm none"

Wicca believes in harming none. We strive to live with this idea in all aspects of our lives. We strive to avoid killing, harming or causing suffering of any living being. Some Wiccans take it to the point of going vegan. They don't want to harm any animals for their personal survival.

We may notice that it is impossible to live "an it harm none" as a rule. Even vegans harm plants. We brush our teeth and kill bacteria.

Wiccans tend to look upon *an it harm none* as a guideline. Something to strive for in our daily lives.

Buddhists emphasize compassion. Many also speak of and take action related to "loving kindness."

"May the roots of suffering diminish. May warfare, violence, neglect, indifference, and addiction also decrease.

May the wisdom and compassion of all beings increase, now and in the future.

May we clearly see all the barriers we erect between ourselves

and others to be as insubstantial as our dreams.
May we appreciate the great perfection of all phenomena."
– Pema Chodron, Buddhist nun

The above quote from Pema Chodron emphasizes aspects of loving kindness. In a way, loving kindness is a practice of extending kindness and compassion outward to others during one's meditation practice. It can also be a way of interacting with people in daily life. It is more than harming none; it is the providing of kindness and compassion to the benefit of the other person.

A Wiccan can incorporate loving kindness in her daily meditation practice, too.

4. A number of Wiccans (not all) believe in reincarnation like Buddhists

Many Buddhist emphasize a belief in reincarnation. Some state that the goal is to learn our lessons and practice compassion—and ultimately get free of the Wheel of Life. That's when one does *not* return to the Earth to suffer during another lifetime.

Buddhists emphasize the Four Noble Truths—often written as …

- Life is suffering.
- Suffering has a cause: craving and attachment.
- People can be free of suffering when they give up craving and attachment.
- To let go of craving and attachment, one practices the Eight-Fold Path (similar to rules).

Buddhists suggest that in each incarnation we learn how to release our habitual actions that lead to suffering.

My personal belief is we are here to learn lessons to advance our spiritual growth. For example, before I was incarnated, I had a lesson plan. I asked other spirits if they would help me learn these lessons. So, perhaps one agreed to help me learn patience, and another would help me learn compassion. Then, we would incarnate here on Earth and help each other. The Gods are present to help us through our lessons because sometimes such lessons can be tough. The universe creates scenarios that will create an opportunity to learn your lesson(s).

Sometimes those scenarios can be truly hard. No one wants their child to die. People would prefer to avoid landing into an abusive relationship.

I've learned that the Universe provides us with paths to learn our lessons.

Sometimes, the direct route to incorporate a lesson into our being is the one that requires us to endure something horrible.

I heard of a mother whose 15-year-old son was shot and killed by another 15-year-old boy. Ultimately, the mother learned to extend amazing forgiveness in that she was the only person to visit the 15-year-old murderer in prison. She lost a son and gained an opportunity to extend kindness and forgiveness to the kid who killed her child.

This mother's faith in a Higher Power provided her a form of comfort and inspiration.

My own elders in Wicca brought the idea of "the universe flows in the path of least resistance" to my attention. I look upon this as the Universe will find the direct path to help us grow.

To Wiccans: the Gods, other spirits and entities provide support and guidance for us to endure the rough spots of life.

5. Certain sects of Buddhism have no concerns about Polytheism

It is reported that the Mahāyāna tradition is the largest tradition of Buddhism, with 53.2% of practitioners. Some scholars note that Mahayana Buddhism spread so much because of the idea: "Keep your gods. Oh, and they are manifestations of the Buddha."

This leaves room for one to practice a form of Buddhism and be Wiccan simultaneously. That plan might bring you to calling yourself "eclectic."

Blessings upon whatever path you decide to walk."

When we see Wicca in light of other spiritual paths, we have something to be grateful for.

You Are Loved and Valued #6

How to Revitalize Your Wiccan Practice

"What do you do when you go through a rough patch and your Wiccan rituals don't bring you peace, like they used to?" my friend, Amanda, asked me.

I pondered this for a while. One idea that arose is: "Do something positive that is outside your routine."

What is your routine?

When I think of my own routine, I realize that I get up, handle email—and at some point in the day I take a walk with my husband. Certainly, I seek out my cat, Magick. He gets scratched and petted. Then, he comes back for more. I do some writing.

Sometimes, your daily life needs a little pick-me-up. When I can, I like to get my hair done—I do need help to maintain my purple shade of hair. I enjoy the attention, and I relax while the stylist does my hair. Afterward, I feel refreshed and ready to go!

The same can be true for your Wiccan practice.

Pick a time to make a date with yourself and the God and

Goddess. Pamper yourself in ritual, give the Gods offerings and tell Them how much you love Them. Some might ask, "Pamper myself?" How about a luxurious ritual bath?

You know what your Gods like. Give Them such an offering and create a simple ritual around that offering.

For example, you could have an in-home spa night when you provide offerings to the Gods made of Their preferences. Then during the ritual, you can soak in a nice warm tub infused with herbs, while you bask in candle light.

Relax with a glass of your favorite beverage and your favorite food. Talk to the Gods, tell Them how much you appreciate Them watching over you. Listen… breathe… relax…

Break your routine. If you tend to stay in-doors, perhaps, you'd enjoy taking a walk next to a body of water. Several creative people mention that they get inspired when next to water. As you walk, breathe deeply and thank God and Goddess.

These are just a few ways to inject new life into your Wiccan practice.

You Are Loved and Valued #7

Goddess Says, "It's Okay to Be Human"

Here is some good news—some comforting news: Goddess is with you through your entire journey.

"I have been with thee from the beginning; and I am that which is attained at the end of desire." – Doreen Valiente (speaking in the voice of the Goddess—from The Charge of the Goddess)

The last part of the above quote has a couple of meanings to me. "I am that which is attained at the end of desire" implies that the Goddess's love is what you receive at the end of your life. I believe we go to the Summerlands at the end of this life. You get to rest and enjoy time with your family and friends. The Gods will be there to give you love and support.

Another meaning is that the "end of desire" is actually a revelation that it is Goddess's love that we really want. By this I mean, that what we want, including inner peace, joy, fun and comfort, are all manifestations of Goddess's love.

One of my friends recently bought a high-end, new car. What did he want? Some form of fulfillment. A car or a hug is just an expression of the blessings from Goddess. We notice that the car or a hug opens the door to good feelings.

Here is a prayer for times when you're feeling overwhelmed.

A Prayer
Lord and Lady
Give me strength
To be compassionate to myself.
From that well may I draw
The love of the Gods to
Persevere on my path
And be kind to others.
So Mote It Be.

May this prayer empower you to joy and fulfillment,

You Are Loved and Valued #8

How Do You Know the Gods Are Real?

"How do you know the Gods are real?" my friend, Alana, asked.

I paused for a moment. I usually talk about my experience of the God and the Goddess's presence that I experienced during a meditation session—some time ago.

But then, I noticed that Alana was serious. She really wanted to know. Upon reflection, I realized that my knowing that the God and Goddess are real comes from three elements.

1. Experience

Wicca is an experiential faith. We don't tell you what to believe. You have experiences that show you what is real and what is not.

The God and Goddess talk to me—that is, I get a deep inner-knowing about things. You might say that I feel something on a deep level. The God and Goddess guide me and show me the way.

Someone might say, "It's just your brain making stuff up."

My response is that I have evidence. Over and over, situations worked out perfectly when I listened to the Gods. I have personally experienced too many synchronicities that make the idea of "it is just made up" false.

Listening to the Gods saved my life in more ways than one. Also, listening to the Gods helped a friend of mine.

My friend told the story about how he stood, waiting for a bus, when he saw a little boy roll his toy truck. The toy got away from the boy and went out into the street. *My friend heard an inner voice: "Hold him!"* He held the boy to prevent him from chasing the toy into the street. A fast moving bus smashed the toy to bits. My friend saved the boy's life.

My friend listened. I have listened to the Goddess. And yes, I believe in the God and Goddess.

2. Reflection

Meditation is a great tool for you to reflect on what just happened in your life. Meditation helps you understand things on a deeper level.

When something surprising happens, you need to reflect on it—to get to the hidden meanings.

Here are some questions you might ask during your meditation session:
- Is this situation really what I think it is?
- Was it a message from the God and Goddess or was it something else?
- What am I feeling about this?
- If God and Goddess want me to learn something here—what could that be?

Asking these and other questions can help you learn and

grow. You might even help yourself transform to a better version of yourself.

3. Express it out loud and see how you feel

Have you noticed that when you express an idea out loud, it becomes clearer?

Even better, as you talk about your experiences with a trusted friend (or Wiccan elder), you discover what something really means to you.

On our own, we can ruminate on some situation (perhaps, someone caused some trouble for you).

However, to rise to a higher level of thinking and understanding, you can talk out loud about the situation. You might even discover new insights. In your own thoughts and ruminations, you may have had no room to consider the other person's point of view. Or you might be so clogged with anger or hurt, that you cannot consider the situation from the Gods' point of view.

But when you speak with a trusted friend (or counselor), you can "have more space" to discover things you hadn't considered before.

In summary, Wicca is an experiential faith. We have discussed how to deepen your experience through *the 3 elements of Experience, Reflection and Express it* out loud and see how you feel.

With these 3 elements, you can process your experiences and come to your own conclusions.

Are the Gods real? Perhaps, that question is incomplete. Are the Gods real to you?

Section 2

Goddess Answers, "Not yet."

Some years ago, I felt an inner pull to get home quickly. Waiting at a traffic light, tapping the steering wheel of my car, I knew that I'd do my usual pattern: light changes—and *zoom*—I move forward.

The light shifted to green.

I heard inside a quiet, *"Not yet."*

What? This was strange.

I hesitated. This was unlike me because I loathe hearing a car behind me honking—"get going."

Still, I did *not* press the accelerator.

Another car roared through the intersection.

If I had failed to heed the inner call of *not yet*, that car would have smashed in my driver's side door. That errant car could have killed me!

In conversations with Wiccans, I've heard a number of them wondering about when it is time to move forward or take action.

Wiccans have several questions that relate to getting an answer from Goddess about timing including:
- Take this risk?
- Trust this person?
- Trust myself in this situation?
- Am I ready?
- Do I need a mentor?

In this section, we'll look at timing and being careful about jumping into certain situations.

Not Yet #1

When Can You Trust Someone and Reveal You're Wiccan?

Many of us face this question in some way every month. And … How do you tell a friend or family member about your faith?

We know that a lot is at stake. Telling someone that you're Wiccan can cause you to lose a friend. Some family members even disown a person who confides that they are Wiccan.

You can use these **3 Elements for Assessing If It's Safe to Tell Someone You're Wiccan.**

1. Is the person open-minded?

Can you figure out if the person is open-minded? It can be hard to tell. However, you can carefully observe how the person responds or reacts to details in daily life. Are they quick to judge someone? Do they say things like: "You know, those people always _____"?

Or do they appear open-minded to different or unusual ideas?

Consider these questions:

a) Is there diversity among the person's friends?

b) Are they rigid about their music taste? (If someone rigidly only listens to Christian music and deems all other music as hell-spawn, watch out!)

c) Do they pick one little detail and get loud and obnoxious without hearing someone tell their full point of view?

Pay close attention. Avoid letting one detail push you to jump to a conclusion. Look on gathering an appropriate number of present-day observations. (Some people can mellow with time, and they might become more open in later years.... And some people become more rigid. Be careful.)

2. What is their spiritual path?

Is their religious path extreme? (Do they act like some sort of rabid nutjob?)

Or is the person comfortable with the idea that spirituality can vary by the individual? And are they cool with that?

Pay close attention. Does the person hold to the idea of a "punishing God" or that their book is "the only book, and it is perfect"?

Be careful to notice if the person has a rigid and narrow viewpoint. Some individuals have been hit with false and extreme ideas about Wicca from certain religious leaders (and Hollywood depictions of witches).

If the person has been overwhelmed with ideas to be fearful of Wicca, you might decide to keep your faith private.

3. Is this good or bad timing?

Sometimes, bad timing can truly harm the possibility of safely sharing your Wiccan path.

Let's say you have a parent who is in the middle of a divorce proceeding. Sharing your Wiccan path might work better one or two years after the divorce goes through. How can that be? Researchers note that there is a limit to the amount of stress a human being can take. If the parent already feels betrayed by the spouse, this parent may also think of your leaving their religious denomination as a second betrayal. They might say horrible things (while stressed out due to their divorce) that they wouldn't say one or two years later.

At other times … If you're having a conversation, and the person demonstrates an openness to a diversity of ideas, it may be good timing to share your Wiccan faith.

Be careful to avoid sharing your Wiccan journey, if the other person is under some extreme stress already. This could be like a couple who *avoids* talking about extreme topics after 9 pm at night. They're tired, and only trouble can arise. And, they'll lose sleep.

The question comes up: How can I help the person get to an open and relaxed frame of mind?

Perhaps, you might talk about your Wiccan faith after a good meal and during a walk in nature.

* * *

In summary, making the choice to share or avoid sharing your Wiccan faith with someone can be tough. We've looked at the elements of being open-minded, the other person's spiritual path, and timing.

I hope this helps in your process of making a decision to share or not share your Wiccan path.

Not Yet #2

Keep Cool Under Fire

I heard a saying: "The nail that sticks up gets hammered down."

Jill Uchiyama said that a number of sad nails are driven back to the floorboards.

Chinese individuals mention a phrase: "The shot hits the bird that pokes its head out."

These kinds of sayings bother me.

Many of us, Wiccans, find that we're being pushed to "fit in with society."

My response is this Chant to empower you to stay strong and keep being the true you.

This Chant can even keep you cool under fire.

By moon and sun,
And by all that runs,
By all that is above and below,
May this not be hate bestowed.
By the rivers and the seven seas,

Keep me in Your kind minds please.
By all Your love and power,
Give me Your strength at this hour!
As I so will, So Mote It Be!

May this empower you.

Not Yet #3

Wiccans Overcome Oppression

As a Wiccan, are you feeling oppressed?

Do you feel comfortable to wear a pentacle openly?

A reader asked me a question recently: "How do you get a girl to like you if you're a witch?"

I had a thought: Why does it have to be a big deal about being a witch? Why is this question phrased in this way?

My second thought was: The question arrives with "if you're a witch" because many cultures around the world oppress Wiccans.

The word *oppression* relates to *prolonged cruel or unjust treatment or control.*

Let's look at that detail *control*. A horrible form of control is related to when other people seem to get into your mind and make you doubt your feelings and worth.

Before we go further, here is my answer to that person's question:

How do you get a girl to like you if you're a witch?

"Your question brings up a number of subtopics.

I'll work with a couple of ideas.

a) How do you get anyone to like you if they might be repelled by a false idea?

You may have heard of the idea "be yourself." Which self are we talking about? The self that has bad breath and a hangover on a Saturday morning? Or the self that you're proud of. The one that is a good listener. Someone who is respectful, kind and compassionate. The self that is open to learning new ideas and approaches—with each day as a fresh opportunity to grow, learn and be kind.

I'm suggesting that you first express your best self. Be a good listener. Be kind, compassionate and friendly. Show a genuine smile at certain moments. These elements are attractive.

I have a friend who asked this question: "If you deal with clinical depression symptoms, do you tell someone that on the first date?" His answer is *no*. Because the person hasn't experienced your good points, and they have no investment in your friendship yet.

When you feel it is appropriate, you might share some part of your spiritual path. Still, be careful because there is a lot of false information about witches in popular culture.

b) How does one use magick to make oneself attractive?

First, my Wiccan elders have emphasized that using magick on anyone without their consent is Wrong—do NOT do it.

However, you can use magick *on yourself* to remove blocks. You might have endured parental neglect or maybe you suffered heartrending rejection. Therefore, you could do a spell to enhance your personal strength. To be a good friend, you need to have the strength to be a good listener and to share your heart. That's right—friendship requires us to be strong enough to be vulnerable with the right person.

Prayer for Strength
Lord of the Sun grant me your strength and wisdom
to hear what is not said,
and to see what is not shown
for my heart is alone.
May I feel your strength from above
so I grow and attract life-giving love.

May this prayer empower you.

* * * * * *

As we close this conversation here, I want to emphasize that oppression happens when people are afraid of something or don't understand something.

Yes—plenty of people retain false ideas about Wicca due to popular culture and to some religious leaders actively spreading false information.

However, we can get to know people one at a time. When they know us as a warm, kind, friendly person, they may be more open to learning who we, Wiccans, are.

Most importantly, stay vigilant about what's in your own mind.

This reminds me of a quote:

All truth passes through three stages. First, it is ridiculed. Second, it is violently opposed. Third, it is accepted as being self-evident. – Arthur Schopenhauer

Not Yet #4

How to Say *No* — and Enhance Your Wiccan Practice

"I wish I could tell people *no*," my friend, Jill, said. "But I'm afraid it's just going to cause more trouble." How does a Wiccan say no and still protect her relationships?

The answer lives in *The Three Aspects of the Goddess*. Many of us have heard of the Maiden, Mother and Crone. I'm suggesting here that all three aspects are necessary—not only for our spiritual growth, but also for us to support our relationships at work and with family.

Recently, I heard multiple times in the same week, Wiccans saying, "I don't have time for my spiritual practice." With people demanding your time and effort, it can feel almost impossible to have time for your personal, spiritual journey.

Some authors suggest that *saying no* is a prime, time-management tool.

I'll add that you cannot merely say *no*. You need to add

something kind and conscious to that process.

Three Aspects of the Goddess

We'll focus on The Three Aspects of the Goddess to help you find more time, so you can improve your own Wiccan practice.

First, you don't just say *no*.

I once heard a speech in which the person said, "You could say something like this: 'I'll have to say *no* at this time. My plate is full. Let's see if we can brainstorm for a moment. Maybe, I know someone who can help you with that.'" The speaker's point was that you don't just say *no*. **You also find a way to be helpful.**

That's the essence of the below **Three Aspects of the Goddess Elements to Say *No* Process:**

1. **Maiden (fertility of ideas)**

Many times, people can be demanding of your time and efforts even when it's *not* your duty or job description.

Still, you need to protect the relationship.

This is the time to invoke the Maiden form of the Goddess, known for fertility. Let's add the thought: fertility in terms of creating new ideas.

When you embody "Maiden energy," you say things like:
- I hear you. The paperwork is tough. How about I brainstorm with you about when in the shift you can do it?
- I understand. The paperwork is complicated. I realize that at some time (maybe I'm on vacation), you'd need to take care of it. When can we take 15 minutes, and I'll show you how to do Part One of the paperwork?

This process is about you helping the person think of ways to fulfill the task or request without you.

The Maiden has lots of youthful energy. To guard your own energy, you need to express to the person what you're willing to do, and more importantly what you're *not* willing to do.

Remember, there are things you cannot do for the person you care about. You cannot take their final exam, and you cannot, in their place, arrive on time for work.

I've heard Wiccans complain about "where did my energy go?" Guard your own Maiden energy by shifting to helping people do their own tasks.

2. Mother (nurture the person to do things)

Embrace and nurture the person. Help the person do things for themselves.

My friend, Jill, at work, puts forth the idea of a rotating schedule for the duty of filling out the paperwork.

Jill discovers that helping the other people learn how to do paperwork gives them a sense of accomplishment that they are growing their skills.

Make sure you nurture (and reinforce) the new behaviors by giving specific praise to another person who is learning new things. Appreciate them and give them good feelings. Celebrate that the person's skills and experiences have expanded.

My husband's coach talks about "growing your comfort zone."

An effective mother does *not* do all the tasks. She empowers her family to add new skills. The family members "grow their comfort zone."

3. Crone (provide "wisdom with a hug")

I think of the effective Crone as one who provides wisdom with a hug.

Without a hug or giving a person good feelings, it's just someone telling another person what to do.

For example, some male individuals say, "I'm a recovering Mr. Fix It." This is recognizing that we want to avoid just telling someone: "To fix that, you should do _____."

Wisdom with a hug means "you hold them and their feelings." And that means you listen.

* * *

In summary, you can create more time for yourself and your spiritual path when you learn to say *no* and add The Three Aspects of the Goddess. I'm *not* saying this is easy. It takes practice.

When you're not running around doing everyone else's work, you can have time for your personal spiritual practices.

May this process create more peace and joy in your life.

Not Yet #5

How Wiccans Free Themselves from Limits

"I'm stuck. I keep ruminating on how that person betrayed me," my friend, Leena, said. "If I could just get past this—get beyond this."

I listened with concern for my friend.

Becoming a High Priestess, I worked for years to learn oath-bound rituals to transcend my earthly concerns. It took a lot of work, but with private rituals, I have discovered how to deeply connect with the Goddess.

Wicca is a path of transcendence, which refers to "existence or experience beyond the normal or physical level."

Beyond the normal ... are we referring to positive or negative experiences?

Perhaps, like me, you've experienced some downright horrible events in your life. The good news is that, through Wicca, we can move beyond darkness to that which includes love and light. We have the power to use magick, and we can invite the God and Goddess to help us rise above the darkness of our negative past experiences.

Maybe, you've heard the term *transformation* a number of times. To *transform* is to *change in character or condition.*

I have looked upon transformation as something that requires a lot of effort.

Remember, *transcendence* is something different. As we noted, it is beyond the normal or physical level. Think of it like this: Transcendence can happen in an instant. For example, some time ago, in the middle of one of my meditation sessions, the God and Goddess appeared to me. This was *not* something I "forced" or "transformed." Instead, it was an experience that just manifested. I flowed into beyond the normal or physical.

So, what does this all boil down to?

Transcendence is something you invite, and you do not *force.*

Here is a prayer that you can use to create transcendence in your life by changing bad experiences into good emotions.

Transcendence Prayer
By love and light,
By Old Ones' might!
I ask for Transcendence of my (name of difficulty) in Your Name.
May You take it and make it tame.
That You turn it into love and light,
So I will be all right!
Let there be a shift in me, from darkness into light.
Let transcendence lift me and take flight.
By all the powers of the Sun, Moon and in Old Ones' Name,
Keep me safe and keep me sane.
Keep me above the dark waters that I tread within my mind.
Let me leave my heartache and sorrow behind.
Create growth for me and my life with no end.

Through every hill and bend.
Pain and fear from (name of difficulty) abate,
So I have only a good fate.
This (name of difficulty) does not define me!
It does not hinder or take me!
The love of the Lord and Lady ever fills me,
As I so will, So Mote It Be!

May this prayer carry you forward and help you transcend that which held you back.

Not Yet #6

When the Tarot Gives You a Bad Reading—What You Can Do

"So, I put the Tarot spread down, and then I caught my breath," one of my Wiccan elders told me.

"Then what happened?" I asked.

"I knew that it was going to be tough to express what the cards were saying to my friend," my Wiccan elder said.

I understood the situation. She was going to have to tell something her friend did *not* want to hear.

A significant number of people are concerned about having to face a "bad reading." It's tough enough to talk about it. It can be even harder to face a tough Tarot reading that applies to you.

Here are three steps to help you work through the dark waters of bad news.

1. Postpone Being Upset by Doing a Meditation
Go into meditation and ask for Goddess's Viewpoint on

the matter. You may be surprised! Some events that look bad at first glance are actually good news.

I have a friend who taught college students. She worked at many different colleges to make ends meet. One day she was doing a reading and saw that she would stop teaching college students. She was devastated.

Then, she did a meditation and asked the Goddess what to do ...

2. Do Another Spread the Next Day

She asked the question "If I do _____, what is the outcome?" When she read the answer, she was puzzled. It gave her the same answer as the day before.

So, she repeated the step of meditation to ask for guidance and to see the situation clearly.

She also talked with her Wiccan Elders and other trustworthy people.

3. Take Positive Action and Add Meditation

The next day she did what she hoped was a positive action related to her situation. She signed up for a Toastmasters group (a group where people practice public speaking)—based on a vague notion that she might become a life coach and giving speeches would help her find clients.

She now says that she gets to work with clients who really want her help—which is quite different from teaching required college classes. She is now free of half-hearted efforts from a significant number of college students. (She hated giving out bad grades.)

So, the "Bad News" that she thought she had received turned out to be a blessing to help her make a transition into what she was meant to do.

Doing meditation sessions and asking for Goddess's

viewpoint can really open up possibilities in your life. Not all endings are bad—although they might include pain at first.

May these three steps help you as you discover your next chapter of life.

Not Yet #7

When do you NOT Listen to the Tarot?

"Can you do a reading for me?" Jill asked me.

"Sure," I said. "What's going on?"

Jill sighed and then asked, "Can you tell me when and how my life will end?"

"That's not a question that I work with," I replied. I went on to share the following four details:

1. **Be sure to avoid doing a Tarot reading when you're feeling terrible.**

Sometimes, the Tarot can mirror your feelings. If you're in a bad mood, you may find that your mood colors what you perceive in your reading. So, your perception can, in a way, "give you a false reading."

I have had to be careful about my state of being when I do a Tarot reading. Why? I deal with clinical depression symptoms, so I need be careful that my symptoms don't mask what the cards are really telling me.

2. Avoid asking about dreadful subjects.

Don't ask: "How (or when) will I die?" And, avoid asking about the deaths of your parents and friends. Why? Such questions put you into a terrible space. As I mentioned earlier, your perceptions can be off, and you might get a "false reading."

3. Don't read for others when they are in a bad/sad/angry mood.

If you read for a person who is in a negative mood, they might perceive anything you say as "bad news." Reading for someone who is upset will not help them. They cannot be open to the messages of the Tarot, and they may twist the news in a negative way.

4. Be prepared for a possible scary or negative reading.

Pause and think about what you asked. Did you ask a question that was phrased in a negative form? If you still get a negative reading, take a break and try again the next day.

Special Note: Let's look at how life goes. Some things seem negative at first but turn out better. A divorce can open the door to a later, wonderful marriage. A friend drifts away and then you later realize that you feel much lighter because you had been in a negative co-dependent friendship.

So, be careful when reading the cards.

Not Yet #8

Beware of Paying Someone to Cast a Magickal Spell for You

"Why are you so concerned about *not* having somebody do magick for you?" my friend, Jennifer, asked.

Three reasons immediately arose in my thoughts:

1. **When someone does a spell for you, both of you become karmically linked.**

Having someone cast a spell creates a karmic link between you and the spellcaster.

How well can you know someone? If you have a stranger do magick for you, then you really don't know the person. However, even if you have a friend do magick for you, you still do *not* know aspects of the person. How is that true? Because each human being has sides of themselves that are veiled to them.

It is harmful to be karmically linked to another person because their shadow self may be intense and can cause you harm.

2. The spell is *not* as effective if you're not the one doing it.

No matter how much you pay someone to care, they won't care as much as you do about the outcome of the spell. They can't. We're talking about your life.

In another section of this book, I emphasize Intent, Visualization, Concentration, and Willpower. These are elements that depend on your unique sensibilities.

3. You do not have a real way of measuring how adept the person is with magick.

I trust that you've met people who talk a good game but do not come through.

We have already established that the best spellcaster for you is you.

It may be tempting to go with someone who charges for spellcasting because they have good testimonials. Still, we know that some people get testimonials from friends who are biased.

Do yourself a favor and become an effective witch yourself. Learn to become adept at spellwork for your own well-being.

Section 3

Goddess Answers, "This is not safe."

Often, we want to trust someone. We want them to help us, protect us or guide us. The problem is that so many of us have been gravely disappointed when a family member or friend has failed to support us in a time of significant need.

Perhaps, you've been in a situation when a teacher or supervisor ignored your safety.

Maybe that person was so self-centered, they did not even know you were at risk.

It is valuable to do the right meditation so that you can hear the Goddess and God say, "This is not safe."

Here are some of Wiccans' questions:
- Should I stay here?
- Do I trust these people?
- Do I need to change my life?
- Is it necessary for me to go into a new chapter of life?

In this section, we'll cover ways, so you can take care of your own safety.

This is not safe #1

The InstaCircle Chant

Have you gone to a gathering of pagans and wiccans—something like PantheaCon? With many magickal people in one location, you might find yourself sensitive to a lot of chaotic energy.

Perhaps, you're like me and feel sensitized to all that energy bouncing around.

I've learned to use shielding, so I can maintain my own inner balance.

If you're attending PantheaCon, you might want to use this following *Shielding Chant* to help you stay empowered in such a highly stimulating situation.

This Shielding Chant can be used at times when regular shielding isn't enough.

The InstaCircle Chant for Shielding

As you say this chant, you will take your power hand, (usually your dominant hand) and trace a Circle three times above and around your head. When you do the movements, you will envision the energy streaming from your index finger.

Soon, you will point to the heavens and pull the energy from there to the ground.

Here is the InstaCircle process with the movements:

Using your power hand, trace the Circle three times.

I cast my Circle thrice,

round, round and round.

Point your index finger up to the heavens and then pull energy down to the ground.

Let no bane get in,
From heavens to ground.

May this InstaCircle Chant process bless your life.

This is not safe #2

Set Your Boundary as a Wiccan

"Are you in the broom closet?" Milly, a new acquaintance, asked. *Broom closet* refers to how a number of Wiccans decide that they must hide their faith. Why? To keep their job or to avoid being disowned by friends or family. I can relate to this. Earlier in my life, I was a solitary witch.

My first response is that I am *not* in the broom closet. I have websites, and I answer questions about Wicca on Quora.com (nearly 200,000 views of my answers at this moment).

But then I thought about this some more.

My husband asks that I keep my pentacle (on my necklace) to be not visible at certain business events he must attend. Am I in the broom closet at these events?

Then I realized an important difference between pushing something into someone's face and answering with the truth.

I told my husband: "If someone asks me directly,

something like, 'Don't you have a blog on Wicca?'—I will answer with the truth."

"I support you," he replied.

My husband knows that I will answer with the truth.

What kind of decisions do you need to make about your own practice of Wicca?

Do you need to make more efforts to gather with like-minded Wiccans?

This is not safe #3

Beware of Mistakes in Casting a Circle

"Can I make a big mistake in Casting a Circle?" my friend, Veronica, asked.

"It is important to focus on three vital details," I replied.

When you Cast a Circle, you want to:
- Keep Things Out—They Steal Your Energy
- Keep Energy In
- Dismiss the Elementals—or They Cause Havoc

1. Keep Things Out—They Steal Your Energy

If you don't Cast Your Circle properly, nearby entities can steal valuable energy you have raised. It gets worse: Such entities can cause your spell or ritual to fall flat.

Let's say you do a Prosperity Spell. But such entities leached your valuable energy. Then, your Prosperity Spell will collapse, due to no power behind it.

2. Keep Energy In

A properly cast Circle keeps your energy all in one place.

When you raise energy, you want it to build—not dissipate into the surrounding landscape. Your Circle helps you magnify such energy.

3. Dismiss the Elementals—or They Cause Havoc

Elementals can cause havoc on your life if not dismissed. I have heard of problems ranging from electrical issues, plumbing problems to scary incidences of fires breaking out in one's home.

Warning: ALWAYS dismiss an entity once it has completed its function.

Finally, closing your circle is truly important.

Just follow the appropriate steps but do them in reverse.

If you follow these guidelines, you will be one step closer to enhancing your life and making your dreams come true.

This is not safe #4

The Wiccan Advantage When Dealing with Worry

"I am so worried," Zoe said.

"Tell me more," I said.

"My whole household is down with the flu. Except me. Well, I'm starting to cough. I don't how much longer I can take the pressure," she said.

Saying "Don't worry" won't do Zoe any good at this moment.

When's the last time you have been seriously worried? Is it happening now?

I've noticed that worry gets more intense about things we really cannot control.

What can you do?

We, Wiccans, have an advantage: We can do an empowering ritual.

The "Let Go" Meditation/Ritual

What you will need:

- One white candle
- Banishing oil or extra virgin olive oil
- Banishing incense or your favorite scent
- Ritual tools
- Cakes and wine

This is a truly simple candle ritual you can do to get some relief from worry.

Cast circle in the usual manner.

Consecrate and charge your candle with your holy water and your incense. Dress your candle with your oil.

Start belly-breathing (taking big breaths in and out—slowly) and light the candle.

Envision all your worry and fretting going into the candle's flame. That is, envision all your worry as a black smoke flowing out of your mouth with each breath out. The flame draws all the black smoke.

Say:
In this moment,
I let go.
Goddess take this from me.
God strengthen me.
So Mote It Be.

Continue your meditation on the candle, breathing out all your worries as the black smoke.

When you're done, thank the God and Goddess for Their support. Let the rest of the candle burn out.

Warning: Never leave a candle burning unattended.

Do the Cakes and Wine ceremony

Close circle

May this ritual bring you relief and peace.

This is not safe #5

A Wiccan Perspective—Grow or Die—#metoo Movement

Recently a reader asked me: "What does the Wiccan Rede *An ye harm none, do what ye will* mean to you? Is it a law, or is it advice?"

If you look at the word *rede* it means *to give advice to; counsel.*

When I look at *The Wiccan Rede,* **An ye harm none, do what ye will**, I view it as sage counsel that is given to us.

Advice fits certain situations. Still, other situations call for using a different approach.

How about self-defense? If you do no harm, like block the attack and cause the opponent's arm to sting, you would be allowing more harm to come upon you.

So, I don't view *The Wiccan Rede* as a law, in part because one cannot live up to it. It is impossible to harm none. We eat, we use chemicals to kill germs as we clean our homes, and we brush our teeth. In all those activities, something's going to die.

The Wiccan Rede can serve as advice to live a good life, to be kind and loving whenever we can. I have found that the universe will return the same positive energy—perhaps, in another form.

I had another thought. Several Wiccans suggest that a principle of the universe is grow or die. If we live by *The Wiccan Rede* as advice, we have the appropriate freedom to grow. As I view material about the #metoo movement, I notice several things. It's reported that the #metoo movement began and continues (as their website states): "The 'me too' movement has built a community of survivors from all walks of life. By bringing vital conversations about sexual violence into the mainstream, we're helping to de-stigmatize survivors by highlighting the breadth and impact sexual violence has on thousands of women, and we're helping those who need it to find entry points to healing."

The #metoo website continues: "Our goal is also to reframe and expand the global conversation around sexual violence to speak to the needs of a broader spectrum of survivors. Young people, queer, trans, and disabled folks, Black women and girls, and all communities of color. We want perpetrators to be held accountable and we want strategies implemented to sustain long term, systemic change."

In a conversation with a number of learned friends, we talked about how any social change has associated pain. Social change does not land in *an it harm none*. People who speak out may lose jobs or worse. One of my friends said, "People, that is, individuals make a decision that the social change is worth the adjustment period."

As I thought more about this, I found this to be valuable: Strive to do as little harm as you can. Be helpful and be kind

when possible to all humans, plants, or entities alike.
This is a positive and enjoyable path in life.

This is not safe #6

Wiccan Perspective: Staying Strong in the Face of a Car Accident

Scrraaapp! A brunch of scratch marks manifested on the side of my car.

Oooh! I got so mad I could spit.

Maybe you can relate to this. An accident. The problem was there were only two elements involved: one human (me) and one pole (it was a *short* pole — one that was hard to see).

This pole collision happened a couple of hours earlier today.

How did I fall into this mess?

It was a confluence of a number of things. I had two friends visiting from out of town. Feeling sleep deprived, I still made it to have lunch with them. Add the hot weather and the sun beating down on my fair skin, and I probably approached heatstroke.

Tired, thirsty and hot, I finally arrived at my car when the visit came to a close. Pulling out of the parking space and feeling really uncomfortable, I was confused as to how to exit the parking structure.

In my defense … I dutifully followed the arrows on the ground near the exit. But the turn was way too tight, and I scraped that damn short pole.

I was so angry at myself. On my way home all I could think of was "You f**king idiot!" I ruminated on how I should have been more careful.

Do you beat yourself up about your own mistakes?

At least back at home, I drank a lot of water. Time to get to the autobody shop. I ruminated again. This time I thought: "It's Friday. They may have already closed for the weekend." I called the shop; they would give me an estimate.

I got to the shop. They fit me in. The tech guy said, "I'll be right back." When he returned, he had two squeeze bottles and a rag. He wiped some liquid on the effected area and slowly the scuff started to come off. I was so thrilled to see that!

Soon all the yellow paint was off, and I gave him my vial of blue touch-up paint. A moment later, the car looked fine. And the best part? It cost me nothing.

I said, "Thank you. I'm so grateful. That's why we keep having our cars worked on here."

The tech guy smiled.

After this, I had some thoughts. What was I supposed to learn here?

What I learned is: I didn't have a buffer. If I had more sleep and had done meditation this week, I could have had more patience for the situation and myself.

When I talk with Wiccans, sometimes, we say, "I know what I should do. I just don't get around to doing meditation or ritual."

So, I just stopped writing this section, and I did a candle ritual—thanking the God and Goddess for the good outcome to the pole collision incident.

What can you do to deepen your Wiccan practice?

Remember, a bad surprise can happen at any time.

We, Wiccans, need to create a buffer in our lives. We need to back off and not burden ourselves too much. We need to preserve our personal energy.

This is not safe #7

How to Hide a Wiccan Altar—If Necessary

"I don't know how much longer I can live in an apartment with those roommates," my friend, Allen, said.

"Something happened?" I asked.

"I need to get into a situation where I'm around people who are okay with Wicca," he said.

I know how difficult living with non-Wiccans can be. Especially if they are *not* Wiccan-friendly.

Certainly, you can't have an altar set up permanently where they can see it.

So how can you follow your spiritual path and be discreet about it?

One way to hide a Wiccan altar is to use a small, hard-shelled suitcase. This is truly convenient because when you're done, you just put your altar tools into the suitcase and put it away. Additionally, your tools are stored simply and easily for the next time you need them.

You can store your suitcase-altar out of the way in a closet or under a bed.

When you're ready to do your ritual (with your door closed!), just pull out the suitcase and set your altar up.

You can even use the suitcase itself as the altar table.

Need to travel or do a ritual at a friend's home? Just grab your suitcase-altar and go.

If you live with non-Wiccans, you can use your suitcase-altar as a simple way to disguise and store your altar until you're ready to do your next ritual.

This is not safe #8

Use Fear as a Positive Source for Your Magick

"Fear can be a Source for magick-working?" my friend, Jeff, asked.

"Yes," I replied.

"I don't understand. I've heard that if you focus on what you fear too much, you'll even attract what you fear," Jeff said. His brows furrowed. It looked like he was making himself afraid by even voicing this thought.

What is fear?

It may seem to be too simple to ask this question. Sure, all of us feel fear sometimes. Still, let's start here: the *Merriam-Webster Dictionary* describes *fear* as: *an unpleasant often strong emotion caused by anticipation or awareness of danger.*

Dealing with clinical depression, I find fear to be my everyday companion. I have fears about having enough income in the future, close relatives dying, and more.

I've learned that I need to do something to get out of the rut of fear.

How can we harness fear?

I've learned that fear can be useful. It's like a warning light (on a pilot's flight deck) that alerts me to danger.

We evolved to be predisposed to fear. Let's face it: Those ancestors who saw a saber-toothed tiger, became afraid, and stayed away from it, survived to pass down their genes. Those of our ancestors who saw the saber-toothed tiger and said, "Nice kitty," didn't.

So, fear is hardwired into our DNA.

This is good to know. We can use this hardwiring to our advantage.

How?

Fear is like a sign that points to what you truly value. Say we have a fear of being alone. This fear of being alone may indicate that you value having friends and family close by.

I fear homelessness. This could indicate that I value comfort and stability.

Finding your fear sign will help you find your way to your true path. Whenever you have fear about something, ask yourself, "Is this my fear sign?"

To Make Fear a Positive Source of Your Magick ...

If you know your fear sign, you can use it to work magick.

How?

In one of my workshops, I had the attendees do a *Transform Fear Meditation*.

The idea was to start with a physical object in your mind to represent the fear.

Then you imagine the physical object crumbling away like an outer shell to reveal what you value hidden inside.

You can use other forms of meditation.

The questions to use include: "What is fear trying to tell you?" and "What path are you to take?"

Look deep. Ask yourself, "What is the fear pointing to?"
For example, one could ask, "What are you afraid of?
Public speaking.
What's that fear pointing to?
I'm afraid of forgetting my words.
What's that fear pointing to?
I'm afraid of being embarrassed.
What's that fear pointing to?
I'm afraid of feeling worthless.

Turn this Around. What is the opposite of that fear?
I want to feel good in my heart. I want to feel that I matter and that I contribute something good to the world.
Now, you have a **Powerful Intention to Use as a Source of Your Magick!**
Next, you can do a *Spell to Boost Your Self-Esteem.*
Or you could light a candle and say,

Lord and Lady, guide me
To strengthen myself
So I feel good about what I'm doing.
Help me to contribute
Something good to this world.
So Mote It Be.

In summary, the idea is to avoid staying in the rut of fear.
Instead, use the fear to point you to a Positive Intention, that is, what you truly value.
Then, have your spellwork focus on what you truly value.

This is not safe #9

How You Can Enjoy PantheaCon or Any Other Wiccan Gathering

"How do I have a good PantheaCon experience?" Judy, a newbie, asked me.

Since this year's PantheaCon will be at least the 10th year I have attended, I had a bunch of ideas rise in my mind.

"Start with the basics," I began. "Enough sleep, good food, enough water, and pace yourself ... oh, and don't try to see everything."

Later, I reflected on the whole PantheaCon experience, and I had more thoughts ...

1. Enjoy What Is There—"Let it be what it is"

"What did you learn last year at PantheaCon?" a friend, Jimmy, asked.

"Enjoy what is there, and let it be what it is," I replied. By this I mean, pay attention to your expectations and how attached you might be to them. If you hold too tightly to certain expectations, you might feel devastated if they're not met. Some people say, "Oh, that ruined my conference experience."

On the other hand, just let the PantheaCon experience be what it is. Yes, you'll find people of like mind and faith at the conference. It can be a great place to connect with people.

But if you're a newbie, you may be held at arm's length by some people because they don't know you. Don't take it personally. After your first year, people will know you. Then closer relationships will be possible.

Enjoy what's in front of you.

My husband tells a story about how he knew a family that always complained about the restaurant food in front of them. It was always: "The fish is more tender at the XY Restaurant" or "I preferred the noodles at the AB Restaurant." Nobody was simply enjoying what was in front of them. That is, the exception was my husband, who would say, "This works for me."

"Wiccans listen to the Earth. They don't shut out the lessons that She is so desperately trying to teach us.... Don't shut out the physical world in favor of the spiritual or magical realms, for only through nature can we experience these realities."

– Scott Cunningham

Just as Wiccans listen to the Earth, listen to your own body. Do you need to take a break? Get a nap? Walk outside and get away from people for a time?

Pay attention to your body and the energies around you. You will learn a lot.

2. Align yourself to your rhythms during the event

Know when you have had enough. Don't stay until you can't think straight. Especially, be careful if you must drive home or to another hotel.

Some people around you may have similar beliefs *and* certain individuals may be upside-down—feeling upset about something. Make sure that you take care of yourself. Avoid being vulnerable to picking up other people's negative energy. In my recent e-newsletter (and earlier in this book), I wrote:

"If you're attending PantheaCon, you might want to use this following Shielding Chant to help you stay empowered in such a highly stimulating situation. This Shielding Chant can be used at times when regular shielding isn't enough.

The InstaCircle Chant for Shielding

As you say this chant, you will take your power hand, (usually your dominant hand) and trace a Circle three times above and around your head. When you do the movements, you will envision the energy streaming from your index finger.

Soon, you will point to the heavens and pull the energy from there to the ground.

Here is the InstaCircle process with the movements:
Using your power hand, trace the Circle three times.
I cast my Circle thrice,
Round, round and round.
Point your index finger up to the heavens and then pull energy down to the ground.
Let no bane get in,
From heavens to ground.

May this InstaCircle Chant process bless your life.

* * *

Honor your own rhythms. Recently, I was reading some material by Doreen Valiente, when I came across this quote:

"This deliberate pacing of the circle is called 'circumambulating.' It is different from the wild joyousness of the round dance." – Doreen Valiente

Sometimes, you want to do a "deliberate pace" and get some rest and other times, you'll probably want to experience some higher energy activities at PantheaCon.

(**Note:** Having a lot of people in a small space like a hotel can spread germs a lot. Consider washing your hands often or using hand sanitizer. It is good to not only put up our spiritual wards, but keep up our physical wards. You'll want to avoid catching ill—something known as "Con Crud.")

In summary, let your PantheaCon experience be what it is, and align yourself to your rhythms during the event.

This is not safe #10

How to Deal with Betrayal when Someone Finds Out You're Wiccan

"I thought I had a friend," Julie told me.

"What happened?" I asked.

"I told her that I trust her with something that, in my local community, I have to keep confidential," Julie began. "I made her promise me—but she told my secret to everybody. And now they shun me!"

"She told them you are Wiccan," I said, realizing.

Have you had a similar situation in your life? Has someone betrayed you and now you just can't get the painful thoughts and feelings out? Does it feel like you're being ripped apart?

To heal after betrayal, we notice a process ...

1. Identify the betrayal

The point here is that you need to acknowledge to yourself that you have been wronged. This person made a decision that caused you harm. Before my divorce, I put up with bad actions of my then-husband. Part of gaining the strength to leave him was for me to put my foot down and declare in my own mind: "This is wrong. I will *not* endure this, anymore."

2. Feel the pain

Acknowledge the pain. Feel it. Until you do, you can't grow and move past it. Additionally, until you feel the pain you might not have the energy to push through and move on. My then-husband would drain our joint account of money to buy his video games and there would be no food in the apartment. He would feed himself with fast food and think nothing of me.

I had to feel the pain and gather my strength to get the hell away from him. (By the way, I'm so glad because after the divorce, I was free to find my soulmate. It's so much better now.)

Perhaps, you're like me, and you'd like a break from feeling so much pain. In fact, I had a recent meditation session in which I asked the God and Goddess, "Why do I have to be in such pain?"

Their answer made me pause. They said, "Pain is to grow."

So, feeling the pain is where growth happens. I know it sucks. But pain is the fuel that creates growth.

3. Protect yourself from more trouble

This is where you need to cut all contact with the person. You can do the ritual below for this.

Here are the steps of True Separation:
a) Verbally end the relationship
b) Stay away from the person.

c) Ground yourself.
d) Cast circle.
e) Do the Separation Ritual (see below).
f) Do the Cakes and Wine ritual.
g) Close the circle.
h) Finally continue to have no contact with the toxic person.

You will need your usual ritual items to cast circle and your altar. As I mentioned you will also have a length of yarn or piece of red string. The yarn/string must be long enough to encircle your own waist and to encircle the object (that represents the toxic person).

The Separation Ritual
Take the object. First, you will asperge it. Asperge means to sprinkle the holy water with your fingers onto the object.
With the holy water, asperge and say:
I cleanse and consecrate you by water and earth.
Next you will cense the object. Cense means to waft incense smoke over the object.
With the incense smoke, cense and say:
I bless and charge you with air and fire.
Then take the string/yarn and cense and asperge it as well and say:
I cleanse and consecrate you by water and earth.
I bless and charge you with air and fire.
Take the red string/yarn in your hands saying:
Tiny bundle of string/yarn, you are now the same as the bonds between me and (Name of person).
Tie one end of the string/yarn to the object and then encircle your waist with the other end of the string/yarn, while you say:

You are the bonds that connect us now.
From me to (Name of person) and from (Name of person) to me.
Our connection is by thee.

Sit and concentrate on the bond between you both and see it as the string/yarn that now connects you and the object. Once you have a firm connection with that thought, take the boline and cut the string/yarn, seeing in your mind's eye the astral bonds being cut along with the string/yarn.

Once you complete the cut, say:

I am now free of the ties of (Name of person) as he/she is of me.

May my happiness expand, and may (Name of person's) happiness expand.

Blessed be.

Finish up with the Cakes and Wine part of the ritual and then close the Circle.

* * *

4. Call upon the God and Goddess to assist with your healing

Meditate and pray to the Gods for strength. Here is a prayer you can use.

Heal my heart and mind,
Free me of violence that binds
Keep me safe and sane from [his/her] madness,
Let me stay centered and stay strong as my own badass.
So Mote It Be!

5. Circle the Wagons with Friends

Keep your true friends close to you. Confide in them and let them build you back up.

6. Move into Inner Peace

Now that you are centered and have had your friends strengthen you, you can now move into peace. You now know that you have separated yourself from the betrayer, and you have surrounded yourself with the love of your true friends and the God and Goddess.

Keep in mind there is a difference between acceptance and approval. You do *not* approve of the betrayer's actions. Eventually, you might get to the point of acceptance. What would you be accepting? You would accept that the person was caught up in their own crap, and you weren't even a fly on their windshield. We notice that people can be seriously self-centered and cruel.

But acceptance is *not* approval. Acceptance is realizing that you went through an event, and today you are *not* ruled by it.

May this material support you and bring you peace.

This is not safe #11

Wiccans, Stand Up Against Sexual Assault

"This is so disturbing. All the rich and powerful men who gang together to protect themselves when we see evidence of their sexual abuse of women," my friend, Jessica, said.

"Yes. And I realize that this is a crucial moment in history," I replied. Jessica and I continued with a significant conversation. From this conversation and others like it, I have thought a lot about what is going on.

Use Anger as a Stepping Stone for Positive Change...

When I was a child, I felt like I did not matter. My brother was given preferential treatment. He tormented me, and my parents' neglect gave me a clear message that he was worth more to my parents than I was. My brother even went so far as to hold me down underwater (at a neighbor's pool), terrifying me because I needed air! His friends, all boys his age, did nothing, to help an eight-year-old little girl. They just watched me being assaulted.

With the #metoo movement and when a woman testified (at a hearing) about the sexual assault she endured, we, women, are now taking our place as worthwhile people who will *not* stand by while such abuse continues in our society.

Perhaps, like me, you were taught to just swallow your anger.

Now is the moment for a new approach.

Use anger as a stepping stone for positive change.

We, Wiccans, know that there are times when we must stand our ground and even actively defend ourselves. During one of my meditations, I used my astral-sword to defend myself.

Methods of Defense and More ...

Here are some suggested actions you can take.
- Meditate and keep yourself strong – Keeping your spirit whole and healthy is the foundation for everything.
- Call Upon the Goddess – In meditation and prayer, ask the Goddess to strengthen you.
- Volunteer in the community with an organization that helps women in need.
- Vote for representatives who focus on women as worthy and valuable. Register if you have not done so earlier.
- Work magick to heal those who have been attacked. This can be as simple as a Prayer to Heal:

Lord and Lady,
grant those who have been wronged by sexual violence
now the power to heal.

May you find these actions to be supportive.

This is not safe #12

Candle Ritual and Putting Up a Shield

With so much chaos in today's political climate and suffering visible around the world, are you having trouble keeping an inner peace?
If so, I'm with you.
This is when shielding comes in handy.
You can protect yourself, and specifically, you can protect your inner peace while the outer world is in chaos.
Putting up a shield around you can keep you sane in an insane world.
How?
A shield can keep unwanted energies from battering you. Think of this shield as a one-way mirror. You can radiate positive energy out but keep the nasties at bay. As I said in one of my posts on my blog: GoddessHasYourBack.com
"Better to Light a Candle Than to Curse the Darkness"
Be a light in the world with acts of kindness."

Here is a simple prayer you can say, as you light a white

candle.

> *Peace be in my heart,*
> *And let all difficulties be pushed aside from me.*
> *Let inner tranquility enter my innermost soul.*
> *May the world's chaos remain outside my oasis of inner peace.*
> *May the Gods provide stability and protection for me on this journey.*
> *So Mote It Be.*

May this prayer empower you and warm you on your journey.

This is not safe #13

How Wiccans Handle Being Betrayed By Loved Ones

"You're no good!" my husband's father yelled at him. This man, I'll call him "George," continued with insulting my husband and me. I was *not* in that room. I was waiting in the car. I will *not* be in the same building as George. George is an unrepentant child abuser, who lost his promotions in the military due to his brawling.

My husband stood his ground. He said firmly, "Stop acting like a bully. You cannot get away with it. I am *not* nine-years-old. You do *not* get to spit in my face. You do *not* get to throw me into walls, anymore."

My husband was visiting his mother, a kind soul.

Do you have a friend or relative who is not only letting you down, but is also actively trying to tear you apart?

Wiccans know that human beings can be complex. Wiccans realize that sometimes you must protect yourself from energy-drainers, or worse, attackers.

Better than this, Wiccans realize that your relationship with God and Goddess is what truly sustains you. The God and Goddess not only hold us up, They lift us higher than we could ever imagine on our own.

The God and Goddess hold our hands on this journey through life and pull us up after we fall and get injured. They hold us as most dear to Them. And when someone tears us down, the God and Goddess are there to lift us back up to our full height.

For example, the God and Goddess can provide us something synchronistic. My husband and I went to a pizza restaurant after the incident with George. And my husband listened to the music in that restaurant. The music felt uplifting to my husband. It was a gift.

The God and Goddess can provide us with inspiration. My husband got a new idea. Next time, he visits his mother and his father tries to derail the situation, my husband expects to stay seated and almost whisper: "Leave us in peace." This just might be a divinely-sent idea.

I've talked with a number of people who have been hurt by others who are supposed to love them. I realized how pervasive this problem is. For those days when you feel betrayed and disempowered, turn to the God and Goddess. Here is a simple chant that will help you feel supported:

"Lord and Lady Support Me" Chant
Lord and Lady let me know,
How this will make me grow.
Keep me safe and keep me sane,
Give me no reason to complain.
Lord and Lady of the Moon,
Give me this a mighty boon.
So Mote It Be.
May this help you when you need real support.

Section 4

Goddess Answers, "Yes, you can grow even if it feels scary."

Some years ago, I woke up around 3 AM—with one solid idea in mind: "You're going to write a blog."

What? I'm dyslexic and I don't have any extra energy because clinical depression symptoms and asthma knock me down.

Doubts rose up. I'm not a writer. I've been beaten down by derisive comments about my spelling and more. During my years leading up to college, I required special education classes.

Still, the Goddess would not let me simply quit before I'd begun.

"You're going to write a blog." The message was clear and ever-present.

Wiccans I know have mentioned these questions:
- Am I strong enough?
- Can I learn this?

- Will someone help me?
- What can I feel good about?
- What can I contribute?
- What is my purpose?
- Can I survive and make a living doing anything connected to something I'm passionate about?

I heeded the Goddess's call back in 2012 when I did begin my blog at GoddessHasYourBack.com.

I've learned that at times, Goddess says, "Yes, you can grow even if it feels scary."

In this section, we'll cover a number of situations in which you learn how to stay strong and step into your personal destiny.

Yes, you can grow even if it feels scary #1

Get the Gods' Help In Times of Disappointment

Today, I was out of the house and helping a friend with her computer/technical project.

Things were going well, and I wanted to celebrate with her by going for a late lunch.

Then *(cue dark-music)*, I get a phone call from a family member.

Looks like I'm needed at home.

Smash went my plan with my friend. My expectation was that I had the leeway to spend more quality time with my friend ... but duty called.

I noticed my feelings. I was upset that my positive expectation had been crushed by "duty."

Could I have put my foot down and told my family member, "No. I have an important thing to do. I'll get back later"? Yes.

But my intuition invited me to return home.

But I was grumpy.

I don't want to be upset this whole day, so I wrote this prayer to let go of my disappointment from my expectations.

Hope of mine that was dashed this time.
Lord and Lady keep me sane,
From disappointment in both Your Names!
Help me release it and let it go
Let it no longer make me feel low.
So Mote It Be!

May this be useful to you—when necessary.

Yes, you can grow even if it feels scary #2

Make the Best Decisions

"I hate making decisions," my friend, Fred, said.

Have you had times when making a decision was really difficult?

Probably, the harder decisions you've faced have had big consequences attached.

We all know how life-changing a career-shift or getting married can be.

Here is a prayer to help you.

Prayer for the Lord and Lady's Guidance to Make the Best Decision

My great and glorious Lord of the sun,
My beautiful and gracious Lady of the moon,
I ask You and the mighty ALL to guide my choices in this situation.
May my anxiety transform into calm in Your loving arms.
May You clear my path of all obstacles before me.

*Shine Your beautiful light on the correct path
I need to take for my continued growth towards success.
Let my decision come to me clearly and precisely.
In this, I do ask.
So Mote It Be.*

Yes, you can grow even if it feels scary #3

Spell for Decreasing Stress

Are you feeling stressed out and overwhelmed?
Or would you like to have a spell ready for such a situation?

Here is a Spell for Decreasing Stress:

What you will need:
- Words that express what is stressing you out
- A virgin piece of paper
- White candle

Numerous people feel great stress due to their experience of worry about bills.

In the following spellwork, we'll use the words "worry about bills."

Cast the Circle.

Light the white candle and say:

Stress, Stress, find a way
To vanish from my sight today.
Stress, Stress, keep away
Not even making a remark, I say!
Stress, stress, go away,
Don't you ever come back my way.

Next, write the words "Worry about bills" on the paper. Then on the next line reduce the size of the phrase by removing the first and last letters of the phrase. Repeat this process until you have only one letter left.

For example:
Worry about bills
  orry about bill
  rry about bil
  ry about bi
  y about b
    about
     bou
      o

Cakes and Wine ceremony
Close the Circle

With this spell, your stress of the worry about bills literally disappears!

Yes, you can grow even if it feels scary #4

How to Do An Extraordinary Prosperity Spell— The Secret of Whole Life Prosperity

"This is the time of increase?" my friend, Adam, asked.

"Yes. We're getting close to Spring. This is a good time to cast a Prosperity Spell," I replied.

Let's look at what *prosperity* is. I don't limit it to just a plethora of money. I am talking about your whole well-being. Prosperity is having an abundance of loving friends, family, good physical health, healthy finances and a good relationship to the God and Goddess.

Have you noticed that having some amount of all these things helps you feel more whole and happier?

I felt great when a sudden inspiration flowed to me from the Goddess to combine the four Elements in a coherent pattern that I call the Four Foundations of Whole Life Prosperity.

Here are the *Four Foundations of Whole Life Prosperity* in the terms of the four Elements/Directions:

Spiritual/East – Element: Air

Having a close relationship with the God and Goddess is key to a good and happy life.

Consider meditation as a helpful way to communicate with God and Goddess. In meditation, you can have your finger on the pulse with the Divine, which helps you create the balance your Spirit craves. Your Spirit needs to be close to the God and Goddess. It hungers for a relationship with Them.

With this strong connection, the other Foundations of Whole Life Prosperity will come to you.

Health/South – Element: Fire

I've thought of the Element of Fire because the Spark of Life, as in good health, supports your prosperous life. Sleep enough, eat healthy meals and get appropriate exercise. After all, our bodies are temples to the Gods. Keep your body in good running order and cherish your body. Nurture your body by bathing regularly and do the rest to keep your body at its best.

We don't need to fall for the media ideas of what a stereotypically attractive body looks like. You don't need to be wafer thin. It's reported that several models are actually unhealthy.

Take good care of your body—as the gift you have. Move in the direction of prosperous health.

Love/West – Element: Water

What does *prosperous in love* mean? I suggest we do what helps us have good relationships.

A friend asked, "What do you think is important to find in a romantic partner?"

My husband replied, "Find someone who is kind and flexible."

I agree, and I've learned that it's important for me to do

rituals and meditation to keep myself strong enough to be kind and flexible. A dash of humor helps.

Taking good care of your relationships helps you support your overall prosperity.

Finances/Earth – Element Earth

A number of my friends complain and worry about their finances. I admit it: I get concerned, too. I'm doing fine, but I have this nagging concern about ending up a homeless person. My husband is ten years older than I am. How will things be after he passes on?

I've learned that meditation and rituals can bring about some peace of mind.

How about you? Would you benefit from doing rituals to enhance your peace of mind?

Doing a Prosperity Spell can bring in some income. Having the opportunity to do something nice for yourself (having a dinner, seeing a movie) can do wonders for your feelings and sense that we live in an abundant Universe.

Putting It All Together

Bringing together Spirit, health, love and appropriate finances enhances your experience of a whole and happy life.

Use this following is a spell to help you move forward.

The Whole Life Prosperity Spell
What you will need:
- Altar and regular ritual tools
- Small pebble (North)
- Unused easy light match (south)
- Thimble of water (West)
- Incense cone and holder (Air)

Do this spell on a waxing moon, closest to the full moon. Focus on this spell to enhance prosperity in various facets of your life.

Cast Circle in the normal manner.

After cleansing and consecrating the items representing the Four Elements, place the items on the cardinal points of the altar.

Meditate on your life being full of what you desire. Once you have a firm feeling about what you want, continue with the next steps.

Light the match on the rock, and say:

Fire burns in my veins with health,

Dip index finger into the thimble of water, touch the water to your lips, and say:

Water surrounds me with the love I desire,

Tap the rock three times, and say:

Earth provides that I am financially secure, and I enjoy financial abundance,

Light incense from the working candle, and say:

And Air sends this spell and my love to the God and Goddess.

Do the Cakes and Wine Ceremony

Close your Circle.

May this Prosperity Spell enhance your life and happiness.

Yes, you can grow even if it feels scary #5

Wiccans Claim Their Real Freedom

When do we really have freedom?
I've learned that it is hard to make a healthy choice when you're in the middle of chaos or stress.

So, what is the solution? Make the choice when things are quiet.

Wiccans, I've talked with, mention how they'd like to feel better. In this section, I'll talk about how you can get to a place of inner quiet. More than that, I'll show how you can charge a talisman, so you'll have it available for a stressful moment.

When you make a choice during a "quiet time," you can later, during stress, make the healthy choice automatically. In this way you avoid having to make the choice again and again. (Sometimes, we do *not* have the extra energy to make the healthy choice at that time.)

For example, my husband decided to eliminate peanut butter and apricot preserves from his daily diet. He made the choice once—when he wasn't hungry. It has helped him drop 15 lbs. permanently. I have used *Goddess Style Weight Loss*—a process I share in my book/online course of the same name. I have dropped 50 lbs. so far.

Charging Your Talisman

Often, Wiccans choose a talisman that can fit into their pocket.
Some suggestions include:
- A worry stone
- A crystal or mineral that is smooth to the touch
- A piece of smooth and sanded wood

Pick something that helps you feel comforted.

Charging and Using Your Talisman Ritual
What you will need:
- Your talisman
- Brown chime candle
- Candle holder
- White candles
- White bath robe (or a different color that you prefer)
- White fresh bath towel
- Chamomile tea
- Cakes and wine
- Gardena incense
- Gardena oil
- Relaxing music
- Kosher salt
- Altar
- Ritual tools

What to do:
Conduct this ritual during a waning moon and when you

will *not* be disturbed.

Set up your altar and place your talisman in the middle of the altar. Next draw your ritual bath.

Add your kosher salt, three tablespoons.

Light the white candles and burn some of the incense for the bath. Play some soothing music on a device safely away from the bathtub.

Drink the tea, then recline in the bath water. Feel the soothing water. Close your eyes and envision all the stress and negative energy dispersing and being absorbed by the bath water.

Deep breathe and relax.

Stay in the bath until all the stress and negative energies are gone from your body. Remain as long as you like.

Once you have finished your ritual bath, dry off with your fresh clean white towel. Put on your clean bath robe.

Next, go to your altar area and cast your circle. Then, sit in front of your altar in a comfortable position.

Cleanse and consecrate your oil and brown candle. Then, dress your candle with the oil—from base to wick. (This pushes the bad stuff away from you.)

Cleanse and consecrate your talisman and rub some of the oil on it as well.

Place the talisman in front of the brown candle.

Light the candle and say:

Fear, stress and sadness, I fling you away
During the madness here with me today.
Let this talisman disperse all my worries and fears away,
Replace with calm and peace for me to stay.
As I So Will
So Mote It Be.

Do the Cakes and Wine ceremony.
Close Your Circle.

Carry your talisman with you. When you start to feel overwhelmed, rub it and feel the negative feelings pulled away and into the talisman. Your talisman neutralizes your negative feelings.

Let this ritual bring you peace in your heart and soul.

Yes, you can grow even if it feels scary #6

How do I tell my mainly Christian friends/family I'm Wiccan?

Are you considering the question of whether to go public with your Pagan faith?

Recently, one of my readers asked: "How do I tell my mainly Christian friends/family I'm Wiccan?"

"That's a vital and complicated topic," I thought. "Can I answer this in a brief article or would this be something to cover in half a book?"

Here's my answer to my reader:

Are you sure you need to go public with your Wiccan faith? Many Wiccans stay in the broom closet and are just happy with that. They have real and intense reasons to keep their faith private.

I have deep empathy for your situation—my own parents dragged my brother and me to their Christian church in our early years.

It's important to consider many issues before you do

something that is irreversible.

1) You will lose some people.

Many Christians have been told by their religion-leaders that Wicca is evil. So, these Christians feel terror about Wicca. Doesn't it make sense that several people may react poorly to you telling them you have different beliefs than they do? You may be shunned—for a lifetime. Are you willing to lose some friends and family?

2) Are you ready to go public?

For many Wiccans, the cost of going public has been to lose their jobs and other opportunities because of their beliefs.

In this day of social media, several authors suggest: "There is no privacy."

Many of us have stories about how someone said, "I'll keep your secret," but later that person blurted out one's private information. How do you feel about the whole online world knowing that you are Wiccan?

3) Are you okay with the possible backlash?

Remember, many Christians have been misinformed about Wicca. Those individuals consider Wicca to be evil. How do some people treat those they consider evil? Have you seen the consequences of those who think they are righteous and they're only "punishing" evil-doers? People who are afraid tend to react in a rash manner.

After due consideration ... here are some methods to express one's Wiccan faith publicly.

a) Let the other person start the conversation

I always wear a pentacle necklace. When some people see it, they make a comment. This opens the door for me to explain what the pentacle means. In this way, I'm able to share some of my beliefs and let them know some facts about the Wiccan spiritual path. (**Warning:** It depends on where you live. Since many Christians believe Wicca to be evil, you might open yourself to violence if you openly wear a pentacle. Please know that I live in Northern California where such an occurrence is unlikely.)

b) Start with common ground

"Margaret, I noticed that you're concerned about taking care of the environment," Amanda said. This is an example of starting with common ground. You can talk about how you also have a deep appreciation for nature. You can mention that walking in nature is like going to a sacred place for you. Some Wiccans mention that they have a "nature-focused religion."

Some people who believe in one God say that they have a feeling of awe when they see the Grand Canyon or a waterfall. The feeling of awe in the presence of nature can be common ground.

c) Talk about "The All" if that is part of your Wiccan Faith

Some Wiccans believe that "The All" began the universe. Then The All manifested as the Goddess who gave birth to the God ... and so forth.

A Christian might be able to understand "The All" as approximating what they view as "God, the Father."

d) Show Your Wiccan Faith in Action

Take up an environmental cause—if that fits for you. Here are options: Do cleanups in your neighborhood and demonstrate the positive things about your beliefs. Volunteer at an animal shelter, or perform some other charitable work. In these ways, you demonstrate the life-enhancing actions that you do, inspired by your Wiccan faith.

Please do a lot of reflection. Get some advice from people you trust. Practice the actual words you will use for your tough conversations about your Wiccan faith ... if you decide to cross this irreversible threshold.

Yes, you can grow even if it feels scary #7

Dealing with Depression While Having Cancer

"You okay, Moonwater? Are you sick?" my friend, Lisa, asked.

"I don't know. The doctor took some skin from near my wrist. I'm waiting on a biopsy," I replied.

Then, the next day, the doctor's office left a voicemail for me—a vague message.

But such a fast return call promised bad news. I had to wait the whole weekend until I could get someone on the phone. The answer was ... cancer.

Now the question was ... did they cut away all of the cancerous cells? The afflicted spot was the size of a dime, and the doctor had used a dermablade to cut away a nickel-sized area.

Again—it was about waiting to find out.

Can you relate? Have you had anxiety waiting for news related to something you had no control over?

Let's add depression to the mix of anxiety and cancer.

My depression symptoms already pushed me to see a

bleak future. Now, with the cancer-diagnosis, my mind spiraled into dark corners. Fear, dread, pain.

So, what can we do to sooth these feelings?

Here are **Three Practical Ways to Soothe Feelings of Dread:**

1. Talk with Friends

You can circle the wagons with your friends/family.

You'll want to be selective about with whom you share your difficult news. I even have a kind friend who prefers texting to talking on the phone. We had a good conversation.

Still, many of us find talking on the phone or visiting in-person to be more helpful.

Many times, your friends and family can be supportive and give you strength. This includes your coven mates if you are in a coven.

A select number of your friends can and will support you. You can lean on them when life gets tough.

Certain friends helped me see the light when depression only showed darkness.

My husband gave me a different perspective. He called the operation a "cancer event." (I didn't like this phrase.)

His point was that the operation was likely successful. So, the situation was over (like an event). He added, "Until the data is in, it's good." By this he meant, if you don't have an indication otherwise, carry on as if you're going to get good news. Sometimes, he calls it "postponing worry that might prove unnecessary."

Some people may find this perspective useful at times.

One thing I like about my husband's comment is that it's about holding a positive thought and sending that positive thought as energy into the universe.

2. Pray to the God and Goddess

I talked a lot to the God and Goddess. I asked Them to postpone my worries until I had more information. They sat with me in my fear and comforted me. They quieted my fears.

I said, "Please let this be okay. Give me guidance. Let me have the strength to go through this situation." I focused on these intentions with the God and Goddess. This provided me a whole different direction than my depression symptoms would have brought to me.

So, when you have a serious question with no answer and you feel anxious, talk to the God and Goddess. See if you feel a subtle shift inside. That would be the God and Goddess providing you subtle support.

3. Perform a Ritual

Do a simple candle ritual to calm and reassure yourself.

I find lighting a candle and asking for peace/faith/comfort really helps me.

You can say:
With this Candle
I honor You, God and Goddess
Please fill me with Light.
Lend me Your Might.
So Mote It Be.

May these above practices bring you comfort and healing.

Yes, you can grow even if it feels scary #8

Wiccans and Psychic and Spiritual Protection?

A reader asked me: "What are some of the quickest, easiest ways for psychic and spiritual protection?"

I'll share three different methods you can use to protect yourself. (We realize that many possible methods of protection exist.)

Protection Method #1: Use a Sigil

Sigils are magickal symbols that hold an intention. You create a sigil by using the following simple process. First, write out your desire on a scratch piece of paper; you can use a single word or a phrase.

Examples of Phrases Related to Protection:
- Protect me through the night
- Protect me from energy vampires

To keep this example simple and clear, I'll just use the word *success*. Cross off all of the repeated letters in Success. You end up with S, U, C, and E. (You want only one of each letter that appears in the word.) Next, scramble the letters, getting S, E, U, and C (for example). Now comes the fun part: Combine the letters together in an image.

Protection Method #2: Wear a Protection Necklace

Wear a necklace of hematite and amethyst. The hematite grounds you, and the amethyst turns all energy into white light.

Protection Method #3: Take a Ritual Bath

Ritual bathing can be a great way to get rid of the nasties that may cling onto your aura. Bless and consecrate your soap and shampoo. Set these aside for use only during your ritual baths.

How to make a sachet with cleansing herbs for a bath:

Use a stocking or cotton cloth, and place inside selected cleansing herbs. The total amount of all herbs will be one tablespoon.

If you use a cotton cloth, gather the corners and tie them with a string. Make sure the sachet is closed and secure. This keeps the herbs from clogging your drain.

Place your sachet in the bath water then sprinkle in some sea salt and let steep for 5 or so minutes. Then enjoy.

May these three protection methods bring you comfort.

Additional Practice: "Fine-Tune" Your Intuition

"How can I practice tuning my intuition?" one of my readers asked. "Are there any spells that can help me become a little more 'fine-tuned' to other people's intent, lies, etc.?"

So much is going on in this question.

First, what is intuition, really? Some definitions of *intuition* emphasize: "the ability when ... one knows or considers [true] from instinctive feeling rather than conscious reasoning."

Researcher Gerd Gigerenzer suggests that intuition is "data that has not risen to the conscious level."

When I talk with fellow Wiccans, I have mentioned, "There is a difference between intuition and knowing." The way I define *knowing* is: Certainty that arises from hearing the 'voice' of the God and Goddess. I've been grateful to hear the voice of the Goddess—on a number of occasions. Earlier in this book, I mentioned the time I had a knowing to hold back and avoid entering a traffic intersection. That knowing saved my life because another car careened through the intersection at great speed. It surely would have smashed my car on the driver's side, killing me.

Next, we look at "fine-tuning intuition." I suggest that this is about getting distractions out of the way so we can clearly connect with intuition.

Gavin de Becker, author of *The Gift of Fear*, points out that we naturally can use our gut instincts to protect ourselves. The problem arises when we let other voices (like when someone doesn't want to be embarrassed) to block out the voice of intuition (or gut instincts).

So, here is a **Spell for Getting Distractions Out of the Way of Your Intuition.**

Intuition Spell
What you will need:
- Blue candle
- Ritual tools
- Dragon's blood incense
- Cakes and wine
- Offering dishes
- Dragon's blood oil

Cast Circle in the usual manner.

Time to dress your candle: This means that you take the oil and rub it onto the candle from wick to the base of the candle.

Place the candle in the holder.

As you light the candle, say:

Blue candle of mine,
It is now your time.
My intuition grows as you melt away,
My intuition is here,
My intuition is clear, and now will stay.
Whispers I hear,
Intuition is near.
Guide me true.
Without distraction,
I know you.

Sit and expand your senses. Sense the whispers of intuition.

Do the Cakes and Wine Ceremony.

Close the Circle.

May this Intuition Spell help you walk your best path.
Blessings upon your journey.

Yes, you can grow even if it feels scary #9

How You Can Do Real Magic

"How can I do real magic?" one of my readers asked.

Magick has many facets. Real magick (spelled with a "k") takes years of practice and dedication to do it correctly. Magick is the process of using natural energies to create positive change in yourself and the world around you.

Many people start by educating themselves with books. Additionally, I would strongly suggest finding a mentor.

Start by asking yourself, "What kind of magick do I want to practice?" You could consider ceremonial magick, witchcraft (if so what kind?), or another type.

Here is a rundown of magick from a witch's perspective. This is an excerpt from my book, *The Hidden Children of the Goddess*:

How Magick works

Without the necessary knowledge, spells fail. I've seen friends disappointed as their spells went wrong. We notice that many people buy a book of spells and cast away, not knowing the how and why. Spells will do a giant belly flop on you if this is what you do without the knowledge of how magick works in the first place.

Intent

To do successful magick, you need to understand several things. First, you must have an intent. You need to know what you want to manifest. I know this sounds simple, but many people just don't think the intent through.

Let's say you want a car. Okay, why do you want a car? Is it to take you to your job? Or is it something you want to have people envy? Hey I don't judge. But if you just say "I want a car" to the universe, you are likely to get that Pinto down the block.

Let's say you just moved to a new area and you need a car to get you around. You want something nice but economical. You don't want a piece of junk that will break down on you every chance it gets. I suggest you go shopping, whether it be on the Internet or at a car lot. Get to know what you want and like for your car.

When you pick out features, you're attaching specific desires to the car. This will help manifest the car you want versus the junk heap down the block. Refine your image of the perfect car in your mind. Include other requirements you have like good gas mileage and inexpensive repair costs. The more specific you are with your intent, the less there will be unexpected results like getting the lemon down the lane.

Having a solid intent is your first step before you do any magick. Once you have that cornerstone set you can continue with the second thing which is concentration. During your spell you will need lots of concentration and visualization.

Visualization

We'll continue with the process of manifesting a particular car. You can use a toy car as a visualization focus object. As you stare at the toy car, you also use your mind to imagine getting into a real car and driving it. You can even take a number of steps further. For instance, if you desire a convertible car, you imagine the wind blowing through your hair as you drive with the top down.

Concentration

This is the process of focusing and then refocusing your mind on your visualization task. In essence, you concentrate on the object and on the images in your mind that are specific for your desired manifestation. It is natural for the mind to wander at times. When it does, you just consciously redirect your mind to focus on the visualization object once again.

Meditation

Some Wiccans begin with meditation to clear the mind before using both concentration and visualization. Using your mind's eye, view the shape. Now view this shape from every angle. Concentrate on this shape for an extended time until you have it firmly in your mind.

Willpower

The Collins English Dictionary defines *willpower* as "the ability to control oneself and determine one's actions."

Kelly McGonigal, Ph.D., author of *The Willpower Instinct*, wrote: "Willpower is about harnessing the three powers of I will, I won't and I want to help you to achieve your goals (and stay out of trouble)."

When it comes to successfully performing magick,

willpower, to me, means the driving force of desire for some form of change. So, I focus on the power of "I will." This is an important distinction because many people think of willpower as only the ability to avoid temptation.

The compelling observation is that Wiccans, who become proficient at these three processes of visualization, concentration, and meditation, actually strengthen their will. How? Once you do the three processes, you actually enhance your belief, and you push through your doubt.

Realize, you need to will something into being. This includes confidence that what you are doing will work. If you don't have that, your spell just won't become a reality.

You need your will for your intent to be as strong as possible. This is why when we are desperate for something, we can usually manifest it. Using your will is deeply rooted in your desire. Lack of will just creates another belly flop.

I've now shared with you the five must-haves (intent, visualization, concentration, meditation and willpower) for doing magick that works.

The above included some of the "basics." I've personally devoted years to earn my role as a 3rd Degree High Priestess of the Gardnerian Tradition.

May these insights help you on your journey.

Yes, you can grow even if it feels scary #10

Ask Great Questions of the Tarot

"How do you come up with proper questions to ask the Tarot?" my friend, Adam, asked.

"There are three things to remember when asking a question of the Tarot," I replied.

1. Ask yes/no questions

Asking a yes or no question is a great way to start reading the Tarot fast. How do you do that? Use these two simple tips:
- Is the card upright or inverted? An upright card usually means yes. However, an inverted card signifies no.
- Do you get a positive feeling or negative feeling with the card? Perhaps, you have one of these two cards: the Sun card (happy/positive) or the Tower card (doom/destruction). What kinds of emotions come up?

2. **Be as specific as possible**

The Tarot can give you strange answers if you're not specific enough. Notice the difference between these two versions of a question: a) Will I make a lot of money? or b) Will I make a lot of money when I sell my house tomorrow?

3. **Form the question as simple as possible.**

Don't overcomplicate things. Don't ask something like: Why can't I find a man in my city with the attributes of having money, and who doesn't live with his parents? Instead ask: Will I find a financially secure lover? Then ask the questions: Does he live alone? Is he local? Don't ask the last two at the same time. Do a series of questions.

May these techniques be helpful to you.

Yes, you can grow even if it feels scary #11

The Tarot—See the Future—and Beware of the Pitfalls

"Are you sure?" my friend, Laura, asked.

"That's what the Tarot cards are showing me," I replied.

"How accurate is this? Is my marketing campaign really going to tank?"

"As I shared with you before ... when I do a reading, it's like taking a glance at a river that is flowing," I said.

Some Insights about a Tarot Reading

1. **Just because the Tarot gives you an answer, it doesn't mean it will stay the same.**

The Tarot spread of cards that you read is a snapshot in time. If you do nothing and follow the course you're on, at the moment you view the Tarot spread, you may find that the outcome stays the same.

However, if you change your actions, things can change.

This is why it is so hard sometimes to pin down exact

outcomes and the final results that may manifest.

2. Viewing the Tarot spread has an influence on the future timeline.

Seeing the Tarot spread gives you new information. What will you do with that information? Will you apply yourself to taking action to change the outcome? Perhaps, this is your chance to change your future!

Still, the appropriate use of the Tarot depends on a lot of variables. It's a truly complicated tool.

Although an outcome may change from the time of your Tarot spread to the future happening, you may still find the Tarot can prove to be helpful in certain circumstances.

Side note: Usually, the major arcana are things one cannot change, and the minor arcana are things you can change. And this depends on which card is next to another. Yes, I did say that the Tarot can be complicated.

Wiccans use the Tarot for many situations including to help people see their choices, to see what actions may be viable, and more.

Like any powerful tool, take care with your use of the Tarot.

Section 5

Goddess Answers, "Come home to Me."

Do you long for a true home? Someplace safe? With someone to guide you, comfort you and believe in you?

Goddess is there. We just need to move aside that which blocks our view and connection.

Perhaps, you can relate to this: With my own journey of Wicca, I started off in a truly dark place.

And the day came when the risk to remain tight in a bud was more painful than the risk it took to blossom. – Anaïs Nin

I started out as a tight bud pressed down by depression.

Later, I came to see depression as a form of cocoon. The pain and the drain of my energy had me struggling with day to day activities. I was stuck. I was too tired and frightened to bloom into who I was meant to be.

Relief arrived when, in a meditation session, I met the God and Goddess. They helped me cut free of my bonds. I gained the strength to blossom into who I am today. They put me on a new path. It was now too painful to be who I used to be, so much so I had to bloom. It was too painful to stay stuck.

How about you?

Are you ready to bloom?

Prayer for Clarity to Be Your True Self
As the wheel turns,
So, does my desire burn.
Seeing through the tiger's eyes,
Keeps me seeing past the lies.
Lord and Lady lend me your wisdom,
So that I may see my true freedom.
As I so will, So Mote It Be

May this prayer enhance your spiritual path.

I've noticed that Wiccans have these questions:
- Where am I?
- Where are you, Goddess?
- Is it good for me to join a coven?
- Should I join *this* coven?

In this section, we'll explore a number of ways to create the closeness you long to have with Goddess.

Come home to Me #1

How Wiccans Get Close to The Source

"I know what to do, but I don't do it to get close to the God and Goddess," my friend, Jennifer, said.

This has been a conundrum that I have faced in my own life, and I've heard about it often from other Wiccans.

Why?

No time and no energy.

This seems ironic in that holding ritual is for generating energy. It's supposed to uplift you.

It appears that many of us are plagued with some self-sabotaging habits.

Here, we'll address the no time and no energy problem.

1. Do something

Light a candle and say thank you to the God and Goddess. Say a prayer. Read a page from a spiritual book. Set aside 5 minutes for a meditation. Simply talk to the Gods.

2. Invite a friend or family member to join you in a candle-lighting ritual for 3 minutes

This is something that can help you feel supported. If you have a supportive friend or family member, you could invite them to join with you—as you do a simple candle-lighting ritual. You can hold the loved one's hands, and you could complete the process by saying a prayer. Then, give your loved one a hug.

May these methods empower you on your spiritual path.

Come home to Me #2

As a Wiccan—When You're Facing an Invisible Illness

Facing an invisible illness? If so, I'm with you. Why? Because every day I deal with asthma, dyslexia and clinical depression.

Here's More Trouble: Beware of Those Who Shame People with Mental Illness in the Pagan Community

What do I mean by "shame people"? I've encountered people who told me that I do not need medication. Instead, they claim that "a certain herbal tea" will "fix you right up." No. That is a delusion. But what really bothered me is their self-righteous attitude that I was not "believing enough." Now that's what I call shaming!

I do meditate. And I take medication. I have medical doctors who help me.

I have depression and asthma—serious diseases. And it is

B.S. to tell me to drink a tea or think or wish my asthma attack or depressive episode away. This is life or death!

I do magick rituals, and they help. Still, if someone says that I don't need medication, they are deluded. Instead, we must be our own advocates as we deal with invisible illnesses.

Why do the God and Goddess let these things happen?

I believe that before this incarnation the God and Goddess helped us plan the lessons we wanted for this incarnation.

Learning lessons on this plane is about taking the direct route. Sometimes, the direct route involves trauma or mental illness. And we know this before we are incarnated.

The God and Goddess don't want us to suffer. They want us to be happy.

They send help to us when we need it most. My husband—that is, boyfriend at the time—came into my life and encouraged me to get help in the form of therapy and medical assistance. I am so grateful to him for taking my hand and leading me to the help I desperately needed.

Why would we choose an incarnation with trauma?

I'll share an idea: Do you really learn what touching a hot stovetop is by someone describing it to you? Or do you learn faster and understand more completely by experiencing the pain?

The same is true with the lessons of our life. We need to experience the situation to truly learn our lesson.

Then, there is the experience of real compassion. Recently, I went through a "bottom-time" (crying and feeling hopeless). My husband sat with me. He didn't try to "cheer me up." He rubbed my feet. I felt better the next day— Thank, Goddess!

Still, my husband knows that there is no "happy button"

on me. Sometimes, we just need to sit with the pain. I deeply appreciate my husband's real compassion and love.

I realize that we do not ask for pain today. Still, God and Goddess often help us have the experience of support when we're suffering. Perhaps, you'll want to do a candle ritual to remind yourself of God and Goddess's presence in your life.

Come home to Me #3

The Tree of Life Meditation

Here is the process of The Tree of Life Meditation:
[A version of this meditation is available at my podcast Goddess Has Your Back on iTunes.]

Slowly breathe in and out. Breathe in the energy of love and peace (envision this as white energy). Breathe out all stress and negativity (envision this as black smoke). Keep taking deep breaths in and out. Concentrate on the white energy being breathed in and filling up your body with loving energy. Then let go and breathe out the negative energy you see as black smoke. As you do this, release the stresses of the day. Repeat this breathing cycle at least three times until you are comfortable and relaxed.

As your body and mind begin to relax, continue deep breathing and focus on this image:

Envision roots made up of energy sprout from the bottoms of your feet. With each breath, extend the roots farther and farther down toward Mother Earth.

Extend them down through the floor, down past the plumbing of the house, and down, down deep into Mother Earth's body. Go down to Her core, to the center of Her heart.

Once there, with each breath in, pull up the energy from Mother Earth. Breathe out the stress, and breathe in the blue-green energy of Mother Earth.

Pull the energy up through your roots, up past the plumbing of the house, past the floor, and into your feet. The energy feels clean and refreshing.

Breathe in deeply. Pull the blue-green energy up into your legs and past your knees. Pull it up, up into your Root Chakra at the base of your spine. Let it fill your body, going up, up into your Sacral Chakra and continuing to your Solar Plexus Chakra. Breathing in deeply, draw the energy up into your Heart Chakra. Let the energy flow down your arms and into your hands. Feel your body relax as the energy fills it.

Breathing in, draw the energy up into your Throat Chakra.

Concentrate on the blue-green energy filling your body. When you are ready, with another breath in, breathe the energy up into your Third Eye Chakra.

Using your breath, draw the energy up into your Crown Chakra. Feel the energy flow throughout your body.

With another breath in, pull the energy up and out of your head. The energy forms like branches toward the Sky above you. Continue and let the branches flow up to the universe and out into the cosmos.

Draw down the golden energy of the Sky and universe into you. Continue to let the Sky energy intermingle and mix with the Earth energy that is already there. Pull it down through your body and into your arms.

Continue breathing deeply, mixing and pulling the energies down to your Heart Chakra.

Breathe in again, pulling the energy of the universe down into your Solar Plexus Chakra.

Continue pulling in the energy. Let it flow into you. Pull it into your Root Chakra. Breathing deeply, pull it down your legs and down to your feet.

Feel the energy from both the Earth Mother and the Sky Father that is within you.

Now focus on pulling this mixed energy out from the top of your head once more. But this time let it cascade down all around you like a waterfall until it completely surrounds you.

With a deep breath in, take the energy and push it out in all directions into an egg shape around you. This is the Cosmic Egg of Protection.

Keep breathing and as you do so, push out more and more energy into your egg.

Your egg gets stronger and stronger.

And when you are satisfied with the strength of your egg stop and relax.

In a moment or two, slowly start to pull your branches back within you, pulling them in with each breath.

Let any extra energy dissipate through the roots that you had placed into the Earth from your feet, keeping the egg intact.

Now breathe the roots up, and back into your body just like the branches that were above you. Give yourself over to the total relaxation you now feel.

In a moment or two—and when you are ready—open your eyes.

Come home to Me #4

Hold It Together Even While a Loved One Has a Meltdown

How do you hold it together while you're enduring a time when a loved one is melting down?

Perhaps, the person is feeling overwhelmed due to stress and work—or that they just haven't had enough sleep.

Today, I had to endure this experience with a family member. This person was frazzled from lack of sleep. I felt put upon. I was irritated—no, I felt angry about it. I really needed the strength of the God and Goddess.

Here is an incantation you can say to help you look past the distress an unhappy loved one is causing.

See the Light in a Loved One Incantation

Lord and Lady grant me soon,
That patience now be my boon.
Let me be granted passage through the storm,

And now let my frustrations be transformed.
Love and Light reveal Your sight,
To give me all Your loving might.
Let me see the good in my loved one,
Let this incantation not be undone.
As I will it, So Mote It Be.

May this incantation help you in a time of need.

Come home to Me #5

A Wiccan Spell for Happiness

"So, what is it that you want?" I asked my friend, Samantha.

"I'd just like to be a bit happier. Is that asking too much?" she asked.

Later, her question started off a lot of conversations between my husband and me. I talked with some friends about happiness, too.

My thought is it would be terrific for Wiccans to have a spell to increase happiness.

But then I realized that what comprises happiness is different for every person. So, my husband and I came up with a list of *Elements of Happiness* that include contentment, joy, fulfillment and satisfaction.

Perhaps, you're like me and find that you really don't have days when your joyful moments comprise more than 50% of the day. There's a reason in my case: I have clinical depression symptoms. This can be a problem in terms of "Can I ever be happy?"

Do you ever ask yourself, "Can I be happy?"

My husband tossed in an idea: "Maybe, some people have a definition of happiness that doesn't allow them to ever be happy."

We all need balance, and it might be helpful to look at all four elements and then fine tune your approach for yourself—to fit your needs. So, I looked up some definitions of these elements:

Elements of Happiness

Joy: the emotion evoked by well-being, success, or good fortune or by the prospect of possessing what one desires. [This is about moment-to-moment feelings.]

Fulfillment: the achievement of something desired, promised, or predicted.

Contentment: the act of feeling or showing satisfaction with one's possessions, status, or situation. [I've thought about contentment as related to sitting still and feeling at peace.]

Satisfaction: the state of being pleased or content with what has been experienced or received.

Then I set out to create a general spell to help Wiccans create or enhance their happiness however they define it.

A Spell for Happiness

What you will need:
- Orange candle
- Candle holder
- Rose oil
- Dragon's Blood incense
- Ritual tools
- Sea salt
- Some of your favorite food and drink (for the Cakes

and Wine Ceremony)
- Lavender flowers (for the ritual bath)
- Clean towel
- Altar
- Clean robe

Take a ritual bath:

On a full or waxing moon, bathe to wash all the physical dirt from your body. Then draw a new bath and put three tablespoons of sea salt into the water. Soak in the water and think of all the negative energy being absorbed by the salt water. Breathe in and out deeply. Relax... Take your time.

Use a clean towel to dry off. Put on a clean robe.

Next, go to your room and clear a space and place your small simple table (this will be your altar) in the center. Place the candle in the middle of the altar. Additionally, set up your small water bowl, sea salt bowl, and food and drink on either the side of the candle.

Cast circle in your usual manner.

Place the tip of your athame in the bowl of water and say:

I cleanse and consecrate thee, Water, that you are pure and clean.

Put the tip of your athame into the bowl of salt and say:

I cleanse and consecrate thee, Salt, that you are pure and clean.

Put three pinches of the blessed sea salt into the bowl of water and stir clockwise (using your index finger).

Asperge the candle with the holy water and say:

I cleanse and consecrate thee, Candle, that you are pure and clean.

Waft the candle with the incense smoke and say:

I charge you with air and fire.

Time to dress your candle: This means that you take the rose oil and rub it onto the candle from wick to the base of the candle. Carve the word "happiness" on the candle and place in the candle holder.

Put the candle into the candle holder, light it, and then say:

I now open my arms out wide
Perking up my internal pride.
The blues that surround me go away
So peace and happiness are here to stay!
Happiness, peace, and love within
Reside deeply and ever herein.
As I so will, So Mote It Be!

Do the Cakes and Wine Ceremony.
Close the Circle.

When you are ready, place the candle in a safe place and let the candle burn completely out. [Do *not* leave an untended candle. Stay safe.]

May this Spell enhance your life.

Come home to me #6

Wiccans Asking the ALL For Change

"I can't take this, anymore!" Rachael said.
"I hear you—" I responded.
"It's all wrong now. I'm boxed in. I just want to feel that I have some freedom. Freedom to choose."
"Have you asked the ALL for help?" I suggested.

Simply put, Rachael was stuck. She felt she had nowhere to go in her current situation. So, here is a simple spell to gain the help of the ALL.

Read over the spell carefully several times before you do it.

What you will need:
- One small white candle (it needs to be small, so you can burn it out in one sitting)
- Candle holder
- Olive oil
- Garlic
- Robe
- Perfume (frankincense preferably)

- Cakes and wine/juice (This can be as simple as some cookies and juice)
- Offering dish
- Sea salt
- Small table (something to put your candle and cakes and wine/juice on)
- Small jar
- Small bowl of purified water
- Small bowl of sea salt
- Purified or spring water
- Lighter or matches

What to do:

Start by thoroughly crushing the garlic and put it into a small jar of your olive oil. Set aside the mixture in a dark place (like a closet) for nine days.

When your oil is done, do the following.

Take a ritual bath:

On a full or waxing moon. First bathe to wash all the physical dirt from your body. Then draw a new bath and put three tablespoons of sea salt into the water. Soak in the water and think of all the negative energy being absorbed by the salt water. Breathe in and out deeply. Relax... Take your time.

Use a clean towel to dry off. Put on a clean robe.

Next, go to your room and clear a space and place your small simple table (which will be your altar) in the center. Place the candle in the middle of the altar. Additionally, set up your small water bowl, sea salt bowl, and food and drink on either the side of the candle.

Disrobe and sit in front of the altar. Submerge your index fingertip in the bowl of water and say:

I cleanse and consecrate thee, Water, that you are pure and clean.

Then place your index fingertip into the bowl of salt and say:

I cleanse and consecrate thee, Salt, that you are pure and clean.

Put three pinches of the blessed sea salt into the bowl of water and stir clockwise (using your index finger).

Sprinkle (asperge) the bottle of perfume with the holy water (the salt water you just made) onto the candle and say:

I cleanse and consecrate thee, Perfume, that you are pure and clean.

Asperge the candle with the holy water and say:

I cleanse and consecrate thee, Candle, that you are pure and clean.

Spray some of the holy perfume onto you and breathe it in deeply. Breathe in and out three times as you clear your mind. Take your time...

Time to dress your candle: This means that you take the garlic oil and rub it onto the candle from wick to the base of the candle. Carve the word "freedom" on the candle and place in the candle holder.

Light the candle and say:

I ask you,
Who is the lightness and darkness,
Who is the powers of the winds,
Who is the powers of the seas,
Who is the powers of the mountains,
Who is the powers of the flame within.
Who is powers all life and love.
And Who is the Source of all things,
The Great and powerful ALL,

I ask you for change and freedom for the good of all!
As I so will, So Mote It be!

As the candle burns, think of all the freedom you now have as this Spell manifests what you desire.

Again, take your time...

Finally, set your cakes and wine/juice in front of you. Hold your dominant hand over them and say:

I bless this food and drink so that it will keep me strong.

Place a bit of each form of food and drink into the offering dishes saying:

To the ALL!

You can now partake of the food and drink.
Let the candle burn itself completely out.
(**Warning:** Never leave a burning candle unattended.)
Clean up and enjoy the rewards of your efforts.

May this Spell bring you many blessings.

Come home to Me #7

How Wiccans Revitalize When Feeling Overwhelmed

"I'm so tired. I've been working my regular job and trying to do my art on the side," Jessica said, in an exhausted whisper.

"How's it going?" I asked.

"I am just way overworked, and I don't know what to do."

So, what is a witch to do?

What really helps is a *Two-Step Release and Recover Process.*

We've all heard about draining out negative energy. It's also important to take the next step and fill up with positive energy.

What you will need:
- Consecrated, blessed oil (for anointing yourself)
- Two candles
- Incense
- Salt

- Cleansing Herbs
- Nylon stocking
- Lighter

Step One: Ritual Bath to Release Stress and Negative Energy:

Take an evening to just lounge in a ritual bath.
- Place appropriate herbs into a sheer nylon stocking. Use the soothing fragrance of Lavender. (Perhaps, you might find other herbs that calm you.)
- Pour a bit of salt into your bath water. Place your herb-bundle into your hot bath water.
- Light two candles and some incense.
- Recline into the water. Breathe deeply. Close your eyes and call on the Lord and Lady to help you release all the toxins into your bath water.
- Let all your stress drain down and away—after your bath.

Step Two: The Special Ritual Anointing of Your Body to Revitalize Your Energy
- Apply your consecrated oil onto your skin. Visualize that the Lord and Lady are embracing you with positive energy.
- Say aloud (you can repeat this chant throughout the anointing of your body):

Lord and Lady,
Enwrap me with Your Love
Strengthen my body,
Revitalize my energy.
So, Mote It Be.
May this process bless your life.

Come home to Me #8

Integrity in Magic

One of my readers asked, "Is there integrity in magic?"
I replied:
"Let's start with two things

A definition of integrity
Integrity is "the quality of being honest and having strong moral principles (moral uprightness)… and the state of being whole and undivided."

A focus on magick (with a "k")
Magic with a "c" refers to stage magic, you know, the kind David Copperfield does. Then there is magick with a "k," which indicates the use of natural energies for change.

Now, that we have our definitions set, let's return to the question: Is there integrity in magick?
The short answer is yes.
Here's why:
Magick is ruled by cause and effect. What you do creates and magnifies the action and it comes back to you. This is

known as the Law of Three, also known as The Three-Fold Law.

You might say that this, in itself, creates a "karmic balancing effect."

This idea of *a form of balance* relates to integrity as a "state of being whole and undivided." Let's continue with that idea. If you wanted to do a Prosperity Spell to bring more income into your life, you'd want to approach that process with integrity (state of being whole and undivided).

I have seen friends try a Prosperity Spell, but come at it from a "divided stance." They want more income … But they don't want the attention that wealth brings.

Or they don't want to, on a subconscious level, "do better moneywise than Dad."

If you are divided in your goal, magick will *not* work. You need to be whole as a practitioner. Whole in your will. You need to be whole in your thoughts and practices.

What can you do if you realize that you're divided in your goal? Meditation, reflection and even therapy may help.

I can say: "The appropriate and effective form of doing magick has integrity to it."

So yes, there is integrity in magick.

Come home to Me #9

Guide a Lover Your Way

For those of us who want to find love, here is a quick spell to guide a lover your way.

What you will need:
- One red candle
- Candle holder
- Lighter

Light the candle and say these words:

Attract a Lover to You Incantation

A lover I seek,
With a smile cheek to cheek.
From darkness to light,
To hold me through the long night.
Attraction I create,

So I can find my true mate.
Sensual they will be,
For lovemaking will be the key.
Heart to heart and hip to hip,
Come to me at a hasty clip.
As I do will, So Mote It Be.

May this process be helpful to you.

Come home to Me #10

The Wiccan View: How to Know Why You Are Here on This Planet

"So much doesn't make sense now," my friend, Jacob, said.

"I can guess some of what you're referring to," I replied. "Is there something specific that really bothers you?"

"I … I guess. I don't know why things have to be so screwed up. I feel really bad," he said.

This began an extended conversation that left me thinking deeply.

So much of what bothers us comes down to asking "Why?"

And then the big question: "Why am I here?"

I have often looked on the earth as a classroom.

So, then the question might take on a new tint, "What am I here to learn?"

The next thought is: "To find out what you must learn, think of… What triggers you? What makes you sad, scared or angry?"

Deep meditation holds the key to the mystery.

Triggers Meditation

Find a quiet somewhere you know you will not be disturbed. Turn off your phone and choose a place to sit comfortably. Keep your back straight.

[Consider recording the following words on your smartphone, and then you can play the recording back. In this way, you would be guided through the process by your own voice.]

First, close your eyes. Notice that the light begins to fade around you. Slowly at first, then it gets darker and darker. Until you are in total darkness, where you feel safe and secure.

(Pause)

Then, just as the darkness came, it leaves. The light returns, slowly at first. Gradually, it gets brighter and brighter. Notice you are in a new place—standing inside a great temple. In front, you find a large stone altar, and you step up to it.

On the altar's right, you see a large cauldron. Within it, fire burns brightly. It is warm and soothing.

Turning back to the altar, you view three objects resting on the smooth surface. Each of these objects represents a trigger in you. They can represent any belief that keeps you sad, scared or angry.

Picking up the first object, you examine it closely. It is round and light.

(Pause)

You aim the object at the cauldron and continue to feel the warmth of the fire. Toss the object into the fire, and watch as it is consumed by the flames.

Smoke rises from the burning ball. You marvel as you see something in the smoke. Realize that this object in the smoke represents an unknown trigger inside you. Perhaps, it is the source of your sadness or fear—or anger.

(Pause)

Go to the altar. Pick up the second object. Examine it and notice it is round and light.

(Pause)

You aim the object at the cauldron and continue to feel the warmth of the fire. Toss the object into the fire, and watch as it is consumed by the flames.

Smoke rises from the burning ball. You marvel as you see something in the smoke. Realize that this object in the smoke represents an unknown trigger inside you. Perhaps, this second object is the source of your sadness or fear—or anger.

(Pause)

Turn to the final object on the altar. Pick up this last object and examine it, finding it to be round and light.

(Pause)

You aim the object at the cauldron and continue to feel the warmth of the fire. Toss the object into the fire, and watch as it is consumed by the flames.

Smoke rises from the burning ball. You marvel as you see something in the smoke. Realize that this object in the smoke represents an unknown trigger inside you. Perhaps, this third object is the source of your sadness or fear—or anger.

(Pause)

Step back from the cauldron. Notice something that you didn't perceive before. Now resting on the left side of the altar, you find a small silver chest—about the size of a shoebox.

Feel something in your pocket. Pull out the object—the key of knowledge and truth. You find the place to insert the key into the chest. Upon using the key, you hear a quiet click, and the chest opens.

Inside, you see three new and different objects. Pick them up and then find a comfortable place to sit down. Realize that these objects represent three positive truths. These objects are the keys to learning how to grow beyond your old triggers.

(Pause)

Your time here is done. Place these new objects safely into your pocket.

Breathe deeply. One ... Two ... Three. Notice the light begins to fade around you. Slowly at first, it gets darker and darker. Until you are in total darkness, where you feel safe and secure.

(Pause)

Then, just as the darkness came, it leaves. The light returns, slowly at first. Gradually, it gets brighter and brighter. The light is back. Now open your eyes and see you are back from your meditation. You are safe, feeling refreshed.

Your Wiccan Path Continues

As we complete this journey with this book, I celebrate your efforts and spiritual growth.

Please continue your path with me by viewing my articles at my blog at GoddessHasYourBack.com and my *Podcast* Goddess Has Your Back at iTunes (and Podbean).

Let's look at how far we have come. We have explored **Goddess's Answers:**

1. You are loved and valued.
2. Not yet.
3. This is not safe.
4. Yes, you can grow even if it feels scary.
5. Come home to Me.

From this point forward, consider learning more about rituals, chants, tips, and ways to customize your rituals just for you ... and even more material, when you sign up for my exclusive enewsletters. Just go to GoddessHasYourBack.com and click on the link (on the right side of the webpage).

Consider my previous eight books. Thank you.

Blessed Be,
Moonwater SilverClaw

* For an Online Course, see the next page ...

Get Real Support. Take the 5-Week Online Course:

ABOUT THE AUTHOR

Moonwater SilverClaw is a Wiccan High Priestess and member of the Covenant of the Goddess and the New Wiccan Church. She has trained people new to Wicca. Her personal story reveals how Wicca saved her life and helped her strengthen herself to secure her release from an abusive marriage.

Moonwater has been practicing Wicca since 1990, first as a solitary and then in a coven.

Moonwater posts at her blog,

GoddessHasYourBack.com

[with visitors from 198 countries]

She felt called to write the blog and write 9 books even though she is dyslexic. She works with a team of editors. At Quora.com, Moonwater has been listed as "Most Viewed Writer" in the category "Witchcraft (Historical)." Quora.com visitors have viewed her answers nearly 200,000 times.

Moonwater has addressed college students in Comparative Religion classes for over ten years. She leads workshops. She lives with her cat Magick and her sweetheart of many years; he is one of her editors. She enjoys knitting and photography.

Her work is endorsed by Wiccan notables including Patrick McCollum (receiver of the Mahatma Gandhi Award for the Advancement of Religious Pluralism).

Moonwater SilverClaw can be contacted at:
AskAWitchNow@gmail.com
Or at her blog:
GoddessHasYourBack.com

Special Offer Just for Readers of this Book:

Contact Moonwater SilverClaw at askawitchnow@gmail.com for special discounts on books, consulting, workshops and presentations. Just mention your experience with this book.

Excerpt from
Goddess Has Your Back

by Moonwater SilverClaw

CHAPTER 1:
GODDESS HAS YOUR BACK

Would you like your Wiccan path to lift up your self-esteem?

Would you simply like to feel better?

This book helps you actually feel your connection with

the Goddess on a daily basis—even moment to moment.

As I mentioned in my first two books, *The Hidden Children of the Goddess* and *Beyond the Law of Attraction to Real Magick*, Wicca saved my life and empowered me to leave an abusive marriage.

As a High Priestess, I have supported friends, family, and colleagues in times of need. My blog GoddessHasYourBack.com gives me a weekly opportunity to support website visitors from 198 countries.

This book gives us the space and time to really explore magickal practices, rituals, meditations and experiences that you'll find comforting and uplifting.

My journey upon this path began with meeting the Gods. The Gods showed me the true path to self-love and acceptance. Where I saw nothingness and unworthiness, they showed me abundance and a unique specialness that I had.

Now I will let you in on a secret. *You have your own unique specialness that no one else has.* It is yours, and yours alone. This new path is yours to discover and walk. Just like my own path, your path is a beautiful discovery simply waiting for you. Prepare to step forward on this new, wondrous, and beautiful path.

Let's take the next step.

Secret of How to Do Magick

When I first started doing magick it was really hit or miss, most often *mess*. My spell work was just not as effective as I wanted it to be. What was I doing wrong?

If you have wondered the same thing, you have probably done similar mistakes. For example, I'd do a money spell, but I'd just get new problems!

The real problem was, like many people, I just wanted a

big payday. What I didn't know was that this is really the wrong way to approach a lack of money.

Many, if not most, spells written today are focused on the external opportunities or even requesting gifts from the Gods. Focusing on just the external can create new problems.

What if I could tell you a **Secret of how to do magick**—in a way where you avoid ethics issues about money?

I have mentored a number of people about this *Secret*. Now I will share with you this Secret.

A phrase from the poem by Doreen Valiente entitled *The Charge of the Goddess* tells us how to do magick well. But many of us, like my younger self, just don't see it. The line I'm talking about is: "…if that which thou seekest thou findest not within thee, thou wilt never find it without thee."

This line invites us to look within as we approach our magickal work.

Instead of focusing on how to get money from outside sources, focus within. How? Instead of asking for a handout from the universe, ask, **"How I can create more energy in myself to obtain my desire? How can I make myself open to more prosperity?"**

Let's get more specific. …

END OF EXCERPT from the book *Goddess Has Your Back* Available from top online retailers.

* * * * * *

Read an excerpt from *Beyond the Law of Attraction to Real Magick*—on the next page.

Excerpt from

Beyond the Law of Attraction to Real Magick
How You Can Remove Blocks to Prosperity, Happiness and Inner Peace

by Moonwater SilverClaw

Self-perspective: Overcome the Blockage of Not Feeling Worthy

Do you feel worthy of the best that life has to offer? Maybe on the conscious level you say, "Sure. Bring it on. The new house, new car, and a real, loving relationship."

But have you ever sabotaged your chances of getting exactly what you wanted?

Self-sabotage can occur because of feeling not worthy on a subconscious level.

If it's subconscious, how can we deal with this?

Good question.

Soon I will share with you a Self-Love Meditation.

But first let's talk about magick. The whole premise of this book is that there is a way to go about the Law of Attraction with more power.

To put it simply, the Law of Attraction is a form of magick, but people who read an introductory book on the Law of Attraction are often denied enough information to truly make the Law of Attraction work in their own lives.

So, to really make a positive difference in your life, we need to talk about real magick. I spell magick with a "k" to distinguish it from stage magic you see on television.

Magick is a natural power, *not* a supernatural one. Who uses magick? In my spiritual path, Wicca, one is trained to use magick in appropriate ways.

When Wiccans do magick, they channel *natural* energies and create change with them.

Well, if Wicca isn't really supernatural then why practice Wicca at all?

To put it simply, *you want something.* That's probably why you were interested in the Law of Attraction in the first place. Now in the context of learning real magick, you'll be able to fully use the Law of Attraction. And that's good news!

Everyone is different and has their own answer to the question of why practice Wicca. I like to think of religion as a bottle of wine. Let's say you have three different people who all taste the same bottle of wine. The first person points out that the flavor has accents of oak. The second praises the hints of apple in it, and the third enjoys the floral notes. They are all right. The wine contains all the flavors they described. But each person detected something different. Religion is like that. Deity can't be entirely known. So, the truth of it is scattered into many faiths.

In Wicca, we honor the God and the Goddess. If that's new to you, you can substitute the label of Higher Power or God or Deity.

The Gods and Goddesses have helped me, and They can help you, too. The first thing they taught me was self-love.

Before we go further, let's make a distinction between self-love and self-conceit (or being stuck in one's ego).

Self-love is about kindness and support. So, it's a good thing. It is NOT about your ego or puffing yourself up.

Let me show you how the Gods changed my perspective on myself for the better.

One of the best exercises I learned is meditation. Through reflective meditation, the Gods helped me understand how skewed my perception of myself really was. This was a key turning point for me.

One thing you always hear about are affirmations, but for many of us, these just don't work.

First, let's cover what an affirmation is. It's a personal, positive statement. It can be as simple as "I feel terrific" or "I make a lot of money."

For many, the above statements don't work. Why?

A number of people have said, "It just sounds like I'm lying to myself."

Like myself, many people's inner self-beliefs interfere with these positive statements. For an example, if I used the affirmation "I am thin," my brain would object with "No, I'm not. Look in the mirror." It's not true. No matter how hard you try to pound that new idea into your brain, your brain pounds just as hard back.

So how did the Gods help me deal with this problem? They inspired me to create a Self-Love Meditation.

So instead of the uphill battle of an affirmation, we'll use the Self-Love Meditation to work with the situation.

END OF EXCERPT from *Beyond the Law of Attraction to Real Magick*

Purchase your copy of the above books (paperback or eBook) at top online retailers.

See Free Chapters (at a top online retailer) of *Moonwater SilverClaw's 9 books*—including *Be a Wiccan Badass.*

www.ingramcontent.com/pod-product-compliance
Lightning Source LLC
Chambersburg PA
CBHW071313110426
42743CB00042B/1495